1795

D0148937

American Foreign and National Security Policies, 1914–1945

American Foreign and National Security Policies, 1914–1945

Thomas H. Buckley
Edwin B. Strong, Jr.

The University of Tennessee Press
KNOXVILLE

The paper in this book meets the minimum requirements of the
American National Standard for Permanence of Paper for Printed
Library Materials.

∞

The binding materials have been chosen
for strength and durability.

Library of Congress Cataloging in Publication Data

Buckley, Thomas H., 1932–
    American foreign and national security policies,
    1914–1945,

    Includes index.
    1. United States—Foreign relations—20th century.
2. United States—National security. I. Strong,
Edwin B., Jr., 1934–   II. Title.
E744.B824   1987   327.73   87-10905
ISBN 0-87049-539-9 (alk. paper)
ISBN 0-87049-540-2 (pbk. : alk. paper)

for Julie and Sherry

Preface

In describing the American search for security from 1914 to 1945, general introductions to United States diplomatic history seldom mention the connections between American foreign relations and American military strategy and policies. Such literature exists in abundance for the period after 1945, when the relationship apparently becomes clearer to historians. Yet many of the foundations of what came to be called the national security state were constructed in the 1914–1945 era. Aimed at university level undergraduates and general readers, the present survey, one of the first attempts at integration, suggests and describes selected major developments in the areas of foreign relations and military strategy of the United States. While basically approached from a realist perspective, this study also offers an overview of recent historical interpretations. A list of additional recommended readings can be found at the end of each chapter.

Acknowledgments

Grateful acknowledgment is made to all of the many fine diplomatic and military historians writing on this time period. Large intellectual debts are owed to Richard Leopold, Norman Graebner, and Robert Ferrell, whose works stimulated and provoked much thought about this era, and to Richard Burns, whose bibliographical genius has contributed enormously to the study of these fields.

Specific individuals who read chapters of the manuscript include: Joe Millichap, Patrick Blessing, William Settle, Jr., Joseph Bradley, Suzanne Tumy, Julie G. Buckley, Paul Brown, John Wiltz, and Esther

Griffith. We are especially appreciative of the extraordinarily intelligent and helpful comments of the first anonymous reader at the University of Tennessee Press.

We wish to thank the librarians at McFarlin Library at the University of Tulsa, Rockefeller Library at Brown University, Reid Library of the University of Western Australia in Perth, and the Library of Congress.

The encouragement and support of Cynthia Maude-Gembler of the University of Tennessee Press was important in bringing this book to fruition. Katherine Holloway's copy-editing greatly improved the manuscript. Christy Treat, Dorisa Chapman-Buckley, and Vi Curtis typed the manuscript through its various drafts with skill and cheerfulness. The excellent maps are by Anna Schad.

The authors accept the responsibility for any errors that may have crept into the book.

Perth, Western Australia,
and Tulsa, Oklahoma,
1986

Contents

Illustrations

American Foreign and National Security Policies, 1914–1945

1 The Heritage to 1914

On taking the presidency in March 1913, Woodrow Wilson became the keeper of a most successful diplomatic heritage that originated with the accomplishments of American representatives at Paris in 1783. Benjamin Franklin, John Adams, and John Jay secured not only a recognition of independence for the new North American nation, but also an expanse of territory stretching from the Atlantic Ocean to the Mississippi River, from Canada to the Spanish Floridas. To the surprise of skeptics, the fledgling nation maintained its independence, consolidated its territory, and proceeded to new adventures. Fortuitous circumstances delivered Lousiana to the young republic in 1803. The country escaped disaster in the War of 1812; acquired the Floridas by a combination of threat and purchase; secured the Northwest Oregon country from Great Britain; talked, perhaps even connived, its way into a war with Mexico, with the result of the Southwest and California being added to the American domain; prevented foreign nations from either intervening in or taking advantage of a fratricidal war; and purchased Alaska, acquired Hawaii and Guam, and secured the Philippines and Puerto Rico as a consequence of a quick victory in the Spanish-American War in 1898. All of this, and more, took place at a relatively small cost in lives and money. An incredulous Otto von Bismarck could well conclude that there appeared a special Providence for fools, drunkards, and the United States of America.

American diplomats, by experience as well as predilection, evolved a set of postulates to govern the conduct of foreign policy. An American statesman in 1913 could look to a diplomatic heritage that encompassed five major principles: abstention from European disputes; an opportunism in North America that took advantage of European difficulties; hegemony within the Western Hemisphere; continental expansion; and active participation in East Asian and Western Pacific affairs. These major principles were strengthened by six specific applications: nonintervention in the domestic affairs of other countries (with the exception of Caribbean nations); recognition of *de facto* regimes—that is, the willingness to have diplomatic relations with any government controlling a country, regardless of origin or character; respect for treaty obligations; peaceful settlement of disputes, if possible, by arbitration or diplomatic negotiation; refusal to export American democratic ideals by force (not America the crusader, but America the example); and no large standing military establishment. All American statesmen did not support these principles at all times, but departure from them was exceptional, not only in theory but in practice.

Toward Europe, the United States government followed a positive and realistic course of abstention. Two related goals found a home in this policy—the maintenance of political independence and neutrality. The Farewell Address of George Washington in 1796 contained the best expression of the determination to maintain political independence. That message, so often misquoted and apparently so seldom read, stated that:

> The great rule of conduct for us in regard to foreign nations is, in extending our commercial relations to have with them as little political connection as possible. . . . Europe has a set of primary interests which to us have none or very remote relation. Hence she must be engaged in frequent controversies, the causes of which are essentially foreign to our concerns. Hence, therefore, it must be unwise in us to implicate ourselves by artificial ties in the *ordinary* difficulties of her politics or the *ordinary* combinations and collisons of her friendships or hatreds. Our detached and distant situation invites and enables us to pursue a different course. . . . Why forego the advantages of so peculiar a situation? . . . It is our true policy to steer clear of *permanent alliances*. . . . Taking care to keep ourselves by suitable establishments on a respectable defensive posture, we may safely trust to *temporary alliances* for *extraordinary emergencies*. [emphasis supplied by authors]

Contrary to popular myth, nowhere did Washington use the word "isolation" or the term "no entangling alliance," which comes, incidentally, from Thomas Jefferson's presidential inaugural address of 1801. Washington did not ask for a negative, isolationist outlook; rather he appealed for an independent foreign policy tied to an American national interest that might, at times, even necessitate an alliance. Underscoring this advice, the first president also posited that "no nation is to be trusted further than it is bound by its interest; and no prudent statesman or politician will venture to depart from it." Whether active independently or in alliance, each nation, including the United States, would pursue its own self-interest.

Neutrality was the second aspect of abstention. Simply stated, American policy was to remain politically and militarily aloof from wars between European states. This policy, clearly related to the desire for an independent foreign policy, had as its purpose a wish to avoid embroilment in European arguments that did not directly affect the interests of the United States. Americans were morally superior to the bickering Europeans and had more to lose than to gain. A wrong choice not only might involve the United States in European affairs, but also, especially in the early years of the republic, jeopardize American independence and perhaps even national existence.

American diplomats did, however, claim that American merchant shipping had the right to trade, within limits, with all belligerents in time of war. Because the United States was geographically isolated from Europe, it was perhaps only natural that the country concerned itself largely with the rights of seaborne commerce in its approach to neutrality, for this was often the only direct contact Americans had with belligerent powers. In the nineteenth century the United States government developed a loose interpretation of neutral rights which gave it almost complete freedom to trade in nonmilitary goods with opposing sides. That approach, never accepted by Great Britain, the dominant sea power of that century, was to become more and more difficult to maintain when wars became total in the twentieth century. Still, since it was possible to declare neutrality unilaterally and point righteously to a considerable body of international law defining the rights and obligations of neutrals, the appeal of neutrality to Americans remained strong.

If Americans were willing to take profits from Europe's struggles by provisioning both sides, they were equally willing, as the second major principle notes, to take advantage of Europe's unattended overseas empires. A highly developed streak of opportunism ran through American foreign policy. While there was an element of luck involved, it was also true that the United States managed to capitalize fully on its opportunities from the purchase of Lousiana in 1803 to the acquisition of the Spanish islands and Hawaii in 1898; America even acquired its most impressive territorial acquisition, the Louisiana Purchase, without resorting to force. Fortunately the European powers were either preoccupied or unwilling to assume the effort and expense of defending and developing their North American territories.

The third major principle of American policy—hegemony within the Western Hemisphere—found its clearest statement in the Monroe Doctrine in 1823. President James Monroe said in reply to a Russian advance into the Pacific Northwest that "the American continents, by the free and independent conditions which they have assumed and maintain, are henceforth not to be considered as subjects for future colonization by any European powers." Warning against a possible European attempt to resubjugate the rebellious Latin American colonies of Spain, he said that "we should consider any attempt on their part to extend their system to any portion of this hemisphere as dangerous to our peace and safety . . . we could not view any interposition for the purpose of oppressing them, or controlling in any other manner their destiny, by any European power in any other light than as the manifestation of an unfriendly disposition toward the United States." While sheer braggadocio at the time of its announcement, the Monroe Doctrine by 1870 was so within the American scope of power that it required neither war nor threat of war to operate. And, one might note, by its one hundredth anniversary in 1923 it was to become such a part of the American heritage that one citizen—none other than Mary Baker Eddy—took out a full-page newspaper advertisement in which she stated, "I believe in the Monroe Doctrine, in our Constitution, and in the laws of God."

Clearly etched upon the American diplomatic record was the fourth major principle, a policy of continental expansion. Whether rationalized as the need for more agricultural land or simply viewed as an inevitable part of an American mission, its force was undeniably present. When the American eagle spread its wings to full flight in the 1840s, they encircled an empire from the Atlantic to the Pacific and cast a shadow even beyond. One could call it "manifest destiny," as John L. O'Sullivan christened it in 1845, or "imperialism" if that word is defined in its broadest sense as one man's domination over another, or even "colonialism" if one were an American Indian. However defined, it had a spirit all its own. Blind or intolerant of native opposition, continental expansion brought within its orbit diverse peoples, and through the principles of the Northwest Ordinance of 1787, which provided for graduated steps to statehood and an equal status of new states with old, created an economic common market and a democratic empire. The greatest wonder is that with a sparsely occupied land to the north and a weak nation to the south the United States did not take more land on the North American continent.

A fifth major principle of American foreign policy was one of participation in events taking place in East Asia. It is one of the parodoxes of American history that Americans, during the late nineteenth century and after, were more willing to cooperate with the political goals of the European powers in East Asia, where American interests were minor, than in Europe, where American interests were major. While it is true that economic and religious goals in East Asia were more important to many Americans than political ones, the pursuit of those ends led inevitably to a greater participation in purely political aspects, for if China disappeared, cut into spheres of influence by competing powers, the door to trade and souls would close. The quest for markets and missions resulted in neither a large trade nor a Christian China, but the potential for both dazzled many Americans and made it difficult for statesmen in Washington to decide whether the American interest in Asia was of primary or secondary importance.

By 1898 the United States possessed a known and successful diplomatic heritage. Important external factors contributed to that result: (1) geographical isolation from the European center of power, (2) dominance of the oceans by the British Royal Navy, (3) the almost perfect functioning from 1815 on of the European balance of power system, and (4) lack of strong rivals in the New World. Some believe that the

American record was made possible by taking advantage of these factors, that the record was largely unplanned or accidental, and that American statesmen could not have acted other than the way they did. But George F. Kennan in his seminal *American Diplomacy, 1900–1950* argued that early statesmen of the United States had viewed the world realistically and defined American objectives in limited terms and sought goals conforming to realities of power—that is, limited goals achievable within the means of existing American power. Kennan asserted that after 1898, idealists, previously present but not dominant, restructured American foreign policy with appeals to abstract moral and legal principles that envisioned goals unachievable with existing American power.

From approximately 1890 to 1914, there clearly was a movement away from the essential principles, but never a completed one. Presidential administrations retained their freedom of action, did not tie themselves to the foreign policy of any other nation, and did not waiver in their support of neutrality with respect to maritime rights. The administrations did, however, begin to back away from an abstention from European affairs. Participation in the Hague Conferences of 1899 and 1907 was more an acknowledgment of American interest in disarmament and the new American status as a world power, achieved in the Spanish-American War of 1898, than a step away from the old heritage. But the actions taken by President Theodore Roosevelt in calling for and taking part in the Portsmouth Conference, which ended the Russo-Japanese War in 1905, and the participation of the United States in the Algeciras Conference of 1906, which involved a French-German dispute over Morocco, were departures from a policy of abstention. Roosevelt concluded that it was no longer a question of whether the United States should participate in world affairs, for by 1895 the republic was the world's leading industrial power. To President Roosevelt it was largely a question of the manner and degree of American participation; the very strength of the United States meant that its options were no longer limited to those of the nineteenth century. For Roosevelt, a mature nation's strength brought on mature responsibilities. American leaders moved away from the old policies reluctantly, but move they certainly did.

The Monroe Doctrine underwent a subtle and important modification.

In 1895 Richard Olney, Grover Cleveland's secretary of state, brandished the doctrine in the face of Great Britain during her boundary dispute with Venezuela. As he demanded arbitration, Olney asserted that "the United States is practically sovereign on this continent, and its fiat is law." Somewhat surprised, but not completely since the personal hobby of the British ambassador in Washington was studying lunatics and their treatment, the British, maintaining dignity, gave way. During the debate, a Texas congressman argued without modesty that the "Monroe Doctrine is as old as humanity. God was the author of the Monroe Doctrine." It remained for Roosevelt, himself not a modest author, to go beyond an assertion of American interest and to add a corollary to the doctrine. In essence, the Roosevelt Corollary stated that the United States would protect Latin American countries both against their own financial wrong doings and those of European creditors. For the first time, but not the last, the American government envisioned itself as a policeman protecting small, weak nations against predators.

In 1898 a foreshadow of change came in the American intervention in a Cuban rebellion against Spain that transformed American manifest destiny into a clear-cut imperialism of the European variety. The Spanish-American War, which historian Samuel Flagg Bemis labeled "the great aberration," resulted from a combination of American altruistic and humanitarian interest in the fate of the Cuban population, Spanish policies of incredible short-sightedness and pride, a presidential administration's (William McKinley's) conclusion that the American people would support a war, and a group of Americans who envisioned the United States as a world power and acted to carry out that supposition. When news of the first great victory came not from Cuba but from Manila Bay in the Philippines, the pride in victory over the Spanish navy at first obscured the significance of the battle's location, not in the Caribbean but in the western Pacific. In a "splendid little war" the Spanish lost to the conquering Americans. In the Treaty of Paris the Cubans received their independence, albeit under what amounted to an American protectorate, and in a fateful decision the United States took over control not only of Puerto Rico and Guam, but of the Philippines. For the first time, the United States had an important outpost in the western Pacific at the gateway to East Asia.

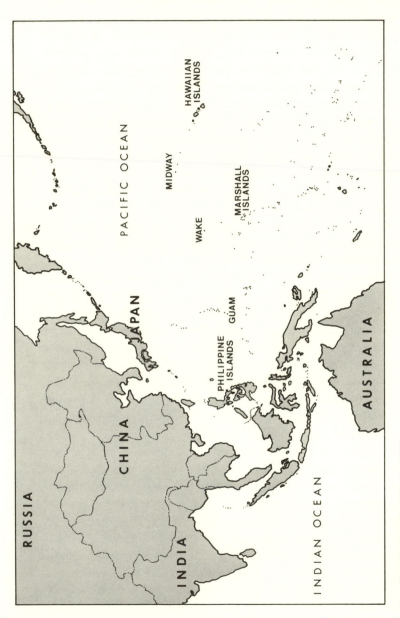

The Pacific Basin, 1914–1945

It was in East Asia that the United States moved most decisively away from its traditional diplomatic heritage. Having generally followed a policy of cooperation with the Western Powers on China, the United States on the other hand had pursued independent policies toward Japan and Korea, as in 1853–54 when Commodore Matthew C. Perry had opened the doors of Japan to the world and somewhat later when Captain Robert Shufeldt took a similar step in Korea. But then American policy in China in 1900 crystallized around the Open Door notes; while primarily economic, those statements also raised political interest to a more prominent position. The first Open Door note of 1899 was within the scope of the American diplomatic heritage because it recognized spheres of influence and simply asked for equal, nondiscriminatory trading rights in China. But the second note of 1900 went beyond any precedent. Secretary of State John Hay announced it would be the policy of the United States government "to seek a solution which may bring about permanent safety and peace to China, preserve Chinese territorial and administrative entity . . . and safeguard for the world the principle of equal and impartial trade with all parts of the Chinese Empire." This was too vague and ambitious and came to be misunderstood and misconstrued by the American people, who concluded that the notes guaranteed China's territorial status and also created a special friendly relationship between the Chinese and Americans.

Noting these movements away from the old heritage, there are present-day students like Kennan, Hans Morgenthau, and Norman A. Graebner, who distinguish between a realistic and an idealistic heritage and find in the latter term a second, more troubling strain in American foreign relations. What do the two terms realism and idealism mean?

The realist, according to Graebner's definition, suggests that the world operates in a nation-state, multi-state system with each nation attempting to advance and defend its security, territories, and national interests. Each nation defines its goals by looking at historic traditions; geographical location; security requirements; and the economic, social, and political welfare of its citizens. These factors, realists argue, change slowly, if at all, and possess specifically defined attributes. No nation, of course, can achieve all it wishes; a nation must make repeated choices between primary interests—those it will fight for—and secondary interests—those it will negotiate for. The task of political leadership is to make that choice. Diplomacy and power are used to advance national interests and goals, defined in such a way that they are achievable with available power. Above all, realists believe that they view the world as it exists and work within that framework, rather than trying to look at the world as they wish it existed. In the final analysis, they are pessimistic about human nature—about the human's ability to solve problems rationally.

Realists found much of their guidance in the practices of classical statesmen such as Metternich and Bismarck. These statesmen believed that beneath the veneer of civilization lay powerful, unpredictable forces of disorder, irrationality, and destruction, which, if not contained, could lead to uncontrollable events and uncertain results. Flexible policies, devoid of grandiose, messianic visions but grounded on pragmatic steps taken with deliberate caution, usually led to mutually agreed solutions, for time and circumstance might change a dangerous situation to everyone's advantage. Such statesmen searched for a right time to act. Bismarck said that "The statesman cannot create the stream of time, he can only navigate upon it . . . he must try and reach for the hem when he hears the garment of God rustling through events." Tradition and past experience would lead the wise man to guide the ship of his country's interests with the stream of history rather than against it.

Wars, according to the classical statesmen, must encompass limited, achievable goals; this excluded wars for unlimited objectives or battles for righteousness. Because today's enemy might well become tomorrow's ally, wisdom advised against fighting in a manner that precluded reconciliation. Despite temporary quarrels and disputes, each nation had a permanent place in the international system; an opponent did not suddenly change to a barbarian outside the pale of civilization to be backed against the wall and utterly destroyed. Wisdom called for forgiveness, recognition of the essential humanity of the adversary, and renewed participation in the states' system where international pressures could influence behavior. Total victory might also bring about a drastic redistribution of power that could well create more serious problems than it solved. A nation's individual goals had to give way not only to the general balance of power, but also to how those goals might appear to others in the system. Absolute security could only come about by creating insecurity for other nations. The ability to place oneself in the shoes of one's enemies, to understand their fears, to see how they viewed your actions, remained important. Room for retreat in any contest, for both your country and for your enemy, became crucial in negotiations to avoid humiliation on either side; most nations would rather fight than lose face or honor. And finally, the use of military power, outside of a threat to survival, must always lead to political objectives. All of these maxims reflected an awareness of the limits of statesmanship, of the limits of military and political power, and of the unpredictability of people and history, for there was no "community of nations" with each nation and culture sharing the same values.

The idealists, on the other hand, generally do not approve of the nation-state system and look to the individuals who make up the nations, not to the nations themselves. They do not consider borders, traditions, and national security interests as having primary importance. They look, rather, to the prevailing political, economic, social, and religious beliefs of their people as the source of policy; such beliefs, of course, are always changing and are difficult to define with precision. Goals cover a spectrum, for idealists speak in terms of peace, justice, freedom, and self-government. They work for a world to come and do not approve of international relations in the world as they exist. Optimistic about human nature, believing in progress, convinced that people can rationally solve all their problems, idealists look to the future and not the past.

Idealists, harkening to the words of the Declaration of Independence, have concluded that American political values, institutions, and ways of doing things are universally shared, in theory as well as in actual experience. This includes a desire for democracy, respect for individual civil liberties, a pluralistic society, and support of a rule of law on the domestic level; on the world level it would include a belief that international affairs are only domestic affairs "writ large" on a wider scale, that there is a "community of nations" that shares certain essential values. All people are basically alike and want progress, development, modernization. Differences in culture are perceived as unimportant and meaningless. A Russian, Mexican, or Chinese peasant, despite greatly varying historical traditions, outlooks and habits, understands and wants the same goals as a Princeton scholar. All, for example, abhor war, as do Americans; people left to their own devices would never fight since support of peace and pacifism is a universal human trait. Thus one would find democracies inherently peaceful. In a world of democracies war could not occur, aggression could not take place, the lion and the sheep could live with each other in peace and harmony.

Like any framework that attempts to divide human behavior into an either/or grouping, the division is not a real one in that there are few individuals and no society that is either all one or the other. In particular, the idealistic/realistic dichotomy leaves out the unique, the fortuitous, the emotional and irrational factors, the force of momentum in history, and, especially in the case of the realist, the domestic springs of foreign policy. Still, it is an analytical framework that has meaning, if only because of its wide use by political scientists and historians in judging the 1914–1945 period, for, as noted, some have concluded that the nineteenth-century heritage was successful because it was primarily realistic and that the "uncertain tradition" of the twentieth century has brought trouble because it is primarily idealistic. At the bottom of the debate is an even older controversy; one that is as old as the human race. That is, what is the nature of humans? Are they basically bad, aggressive, and combative, only restrained by force? Or are they basically good, peaceful, cooperative, dominated by enlightened values? As with the elements of idealism and realism, most likely there are aspects of both within humans. That seems the case with those who designed and guided America's role in the world in the first half of the twentieth century.

Developments in the military sphere, while closely connected to the certain tradition in American foreign relations, evoked less discussion. Except in wartime, neither the government nor the public gave much thought to the military, let alone to military strategy, until the closing decade of the nineteenth century. A colonial belief, reinforced by the experiences of the revolutionary era, held that standing armies posed a threat to democratic institutions. Four major wars—in 1812, 1848, 1861, and 1898—seemed to prove that a large volunteer army could be raised and trained to fight effectively in the event of crucial need. Large numbers of men in frontier America had grown up with guns and needed little specialized training; few unique or complex weapons then existed, nor did they seem necessary. In wartime the "American Way of War," based on attrition methods—that is, the wearing down of the opposition through the sheer number of soldiers and industrial might, rather than by strategic maneuver—worked successfully. A small professional army provided leadership in wartime; in peacetime they guarded governmental and military installations, and fought Indians. Life on the Indian frontier had little romance, much hardship, and considerable boredom along with periodic danger for those such as George Custer who underestimated the foe. With the exception of the Indians, the United States Army threatened no one and, with rare exceptions, seldom functioned as an instrument of statecraft. The lack of an immediate foreign threat on the land borders of America contributed to the growth of the feeling that a large professional army would be a luxury that the United States could do without.

The United States Navy, however, played a more ambivalent role. Based, too, on a small professional corps, also greatly augmented in wartime, then drastically cut back immediately after a war, the navy primarily sold itself as a coastal defense force. Emphasis on defense enabled the navy to gain funds with more ease than the army. Absence from all but major port cities led the navy to a more understated presence than the army, and few Americans ever thought of the navy as a threat to democratic institutions. But the navy's self-proclaimed role as the front line of American defense should not obscure its other use as an active instrument of American foreign policy. From the time of John Paul Jones in the American Revolution, to the shores of Tripoli against marauding pirates, and to the opening of Japan by Commodore Mathew C. Perry, the navy found itself used to protect American commerce and citizens abroad. Ranked a third-rate navy prior to the 1890s and even threatened by a minor power like Chile, the American navy was not viewed by many nations as a serious threat, or even as anything but a minor element in world politics. A rudimentary strategy—cruiser warfare, the raiding of enemy merchant ships in wartime—began to change drastically when the quest for American empire moved overseas in the late 1890s.

The genesis of the twentieth-century security policy of the United

Alfred Thayer Mahan.

States extends back to 1890 with the publication of Alfred Thayer Mahan's thesis on sea power. Mahan became the designer of the concepts of the emerging American navy and the early twentieth-century global strategy of the United States. Mahan's books, and the several articles that accompanied them, had a profound and at times exhilarating effect on presidents, secretaries of state, legislators, and private citizens. No less so, for decades after he wrote, Mahan influenced historians in their evaluation of the forces and effects of American diplomatic and military history.

Mahan's book, *The Influence of Sea Power upon History, 1660–1783,* presented a lucid justification for an aggressive foreign policy conducted with the assistance of military power in the form of a powerful navy. Once a declaration of war occurred, it "must be waged offensively, aggressively." Mahan further advocated that "the enemy must not be fended off, but smitten down." Coastal defense no longer remained the navy's primary purpose; rather an offensive strategy envisioned the navy defeating the enemy at great distances from the shores of the United States. According to Mahan, battleships, not cruisers, would operate as the key weapons. A large, offensive navy needed bases away from the homeland, and it was no coincidence that in the decade following the publication of Mahan's book, the United States secured a variety of islands extending across the Pacific Ocean and covering the key areas of the Caribbean Sea.

This sea power strategy, based on Mahan's view of history and his admiration of Great Britain's success as a world power, had a strong appeal. To him, a nation never stood still; it advanced or declined. To advance, a nation needed commerce, a merchant marine to carry it, and a navy to insure and protect that trade. Mahan, certainly a champion of naval power, also appealed first and foremost to the forces of nationalism. The vastness of the oceans and the lack of other military powers in the Western Hemisphere seemed to cast a special blessing on the United States. Mahan believed that his country could replicate the success of the British, and this led him to see analogies in areas at best questionable. His vision as a naval theorist had flaws, but Mahan's writings captured the imagination of leaders eager for visions.

The presidency of Theodore Roosevelt allowed the Mahan thesis to become navy policy, and by the end of his elected term Roosevelt had created the second largest navy (led by sixteen battleships) in the world. But a real difference existed between what Mahan advocated and what Roosevelt practiced. Mahan viewed the interests of the United States as directly linked to Asia and Europe. Roosevelt, however, had a hemispheric view and wanted a navy only to insure the ability of the United States to control the waters and destiny of the Western Hemisphere.

During the first decade of the twentieth century, several events moved the United States toward the development of a comprehensive national security policy. The Navy General Board, created to define and conduct naval policy and planning, adopted Mahan's concepts and quickly advocated a navy consisting of forty-eight battleships—not to have one named for every state, as critics contended, but in order to create the offensive-aggressive navy that Mahan argued would best further the foreign policy and economic interests of the United States. The board further selected the British as the most probable allies in any future conflict and the Germans and Japanese as the most likely enemies the navy would have to fight. Policy and planning, therefore, focused on the Pacific Ocean, where the United States would bear the brunt of future conflict. The Joint Board of the Army and Navy, a forerunner of the current Joint Chiefs of Staff, gave approval to the navy's strategy. Mahan's thesis provided the impetus not only for much of the strategy of the Spanish-American War, but also for the resurrection of the Monroe Doctrine, the construction of the Panama Canal, the creation of island bases throughout the Pacific Ocean, and perhaps even some of the economic investments in Latin America and Asia. Not ahead of his time, Mahan sensed and captured the spirit of religious evangelism, national pride, and social Darwinism that already existed. So well accepted, he reflected latent ambitions that existed in government, the military, and, especially, in American business.

On the eve of the First World War the United States had a choice of diplomatic traditions and a developing military strategy centered on the use of sea power. It remained for President Woodrow Wilson to decide which policies would characterize American foreign affairs. His choices became crucial, for they came to characterize much of the American outlook on the world in the first half of the twentieth century.

Selected Reading

The best bibliographical guide, complete with annotated listings of books and articles, is Richard Dean Burns, ed., *Guide to American Foreign Relations Since 1700* (1983). A five-volume series, published by the Council on Foreign Relations, *Foreign Affairs Bibliography* (1933–1976) contains annotated listings of books published from 1919 to 1972: its *Foreign Affairs 50-Year Bibliography* (1972) selects and recommends items from the full five volumes. The Council also publishes a quarterly journal, *Foreign Affairs* (1921–   ), which includes a book section listing both historical and current volumes dealing with foreign affairs. *America: History and Life* (1964–   ), *Reader's Guide to Periodical Literature* (1905–   ), and the *New York Times Index* (1913–   ) are other useful guides.

The Department of State's brown buckram volumes, *Foreign Relations of the United States,* contain the relevant archival documents from its files for the 1914–1945 time period. Two other collections are useful: Robert H. Ferrell, ed., *America as a World Power* (1971) and Norman Graebner, ed., *Ideas and Diplomacy: Readings in the Intellectual Tradition of American Foreign Policy* (1964).

Broad textbook compilations, written in lively, provocative styles, can be found in Robert H. Ferrell's *American Diplomacy* (1975), Thomas A. Bailey's *A Diplomatic History of the American People* (1980), and Norman Graebner's *America as a World Power: A Realist Appraisal from Wilson to Reagan* (1985). Nor should one overlook the insights of Richard W. Leopold's *The Growth of American Foreign Policy: A History* (1962), which includes both political and military issues.

The membership of the Society for Historians of American Foreign Relations, publishers of the Burns bibliographical guide mentioned above, also offer other publications. Its *Newsletter* (1969–   ) and journal, *Diplomatic History* (1977–   ), contain historical essays, articles, and information on twentieth-century American foreign relations.

Important interpretations include: George F. Kennan, *American Diplomacy, 1900–1950* (1951), a seminal realist work; Robert E. Osgood, *Ideals and Self-Interest in America's Foreign Relations; The Great Transformation of the Twentieth Century* (1953); and the stimulating economic emphasis of *The Tragedy of American Diplomacy* by William A. Williams. *Democratic Ideals and Reality* (1919) by Halford J. Mackinder presents the Heartland thesis of geopolitics, while Paul M. Kennedy brilliantly argues the Mahan concepts of sea power in *The Rise and Fall of British Naval Mastery* (1976). See also Lloyd Gardner's "American Foreign Policy, 1900–1921: A Second Look at the Realist Critique of American Diplomacy," in Barton J. Bernstein, ed., *Towards a New Past: Dissenting Essays in American History* (1968). The arguments of Herbert Butterfield on the balance of power can best be found in *Diplomatic Investigations:*

Essays in the Theory of International Politics (1966). Last, but far from least, are the works of Michael Howard; his *The Causes of War* (1984) is a most important addition to a growing corpus of thought by a leading British scholar on war.

Bibliographies that stress the relationships between foreign policy and the use of military power are: Robin Higham, ed., *A Guide to the Sources of United States Military History* (1975), which contains an excellent series of bibliographical essays, and John E. Jessup and Robert W. Coakley, eds., *A Guide to the Study and Use of Military History* (1979). Also useful for this time period is Richard Dean Burns, ed., *Arms Control and Disarmament: A Bibliography* (1977).

Walter Millis' *Arms and Men: A Study of American Military History* (1956) is dated but essential. Two works by Russell F. Weigley and Allan R. Millett, respectively, *The American Way of War: A History of United States Military Strategy and Policy* (1973) and *For the Common Defense: A Military History of the United States of America, 1607–1983* (1984), are excellent. Millett has also written *Semper Fidelis: The History of the United States Marine Corps* (1980). Kenneth Hagan, ed., *In Peace and War: Interpretations of American Naval History, 1775–1984* (1984) has excellent essays. A companion volume by Hagan and William R. Roberts, eds., *Against All Enemies: Interpretations of American Military History From Colonial Times to the Present* (1986) offers similar quality. The most useful edition of Carl von Clausewitz's *On War* is the 1976 volume by Michael Howard and Peter Paret.

2 Wilson and War

Woodrow Wilson and Franklin Roosevelt stand at the apex of the major events that occurred in American foreign relations from 1914 to 1945. These two war presidents, both members of the progressive, liberal wing of the Democratic party, eclipse lesser lights such as Henry Cabot Lodge, Charles Evans Hughes, Frank B. Kellogg, William E. Borah, Henry L. Stimson, and Cordell Hull, all of whom shone brightly, but only for a moment. Wilson, in turn, would rank ahead of Roosevelt, if only on the basis of leaving an enduring intellectual heritage. "Wilsonianism" became the center of a controversy of considerable proportions; followers of Wilson's policies and ideas, and opponents who reacted strongly against them, were at the core of almost every major dispute of the period. Supporters argued that he was the statesman of his time, a prophet of the future whose search for the Holy Grail of peace, like that of the medieval knights, was thwarted by the short-sightedness and weakness of others. Opponents contended that he was too much the idealist, too blind to the realities of the world, and too much a true believer in his own powers to influence and direct. Regardless of the respective merits of the controversy, the fact that it was Wilson who precipitated the division and left the legacy is beyond argument.

Wilson, whose lack of experience in foreign affairs prior to the presidency caused him to remark, as if to tempt the Fates, that it would be an "irony of history if my administration had to deal largely in foreign affairs," was to come to some strongly-held opinions in a remarkably short period of time and without the benefit of either deep study or wide contacts. The presidency seldom affords the luxury of weeks and months of careful investigation into problems; nor was Wilson one whose temperament made it easy for him to seek the advice of those of differing viewpoints. To effect the transition from one of inattention to world affairs to that of a leader immersed in world problems, Wilson had to draw upon sources other than those of experience, study, or advice. He turned naturally to his Presbyterian and progressive heritages which had served him in such good stead in his rise from university professor to president. Wilson had successfully applied both in capturing the presidency and pushing through a major domestic reform program. Wilsonianism as applied to foreign affairs is in large measure a combination of Christian moralism and progressive optimism writ large. That he fell back on that heritage rather than the diplomatic tradition of the nineteenth century is of some importance.

Five major ideas lay at the core of Wilson's thoughts as they pertained to foreign policy: 1) a predominantly idealistic approach that stressed morality, broad principles, and the belief that rational persons working together could solve all problems; 2) a belief that God directed the activities of all people and nations and that, as a result, short-term goals should not take precedence over long-term ones; 3) an assumption that the United States, devoid of a lust for power and riches, had a particular mission and responsibility to bring peace and democracy to the world; 4) a conclusion that all people were capable of self-government and democracy; and 5) a view that his ideas and thoughts were universal, that all right-thinking persons in all countries thought as he and desired the same goals.

There were, of course, strengths and weaknesses to Wilson's approach. People the world over have followed leaders who offer positive visions of a better, more peaceful world. Hearts and steps quicken in response to such appeals from leaders in positions of responsibility. His beliefs made Wilson an incomparable war leader for he led an ideological, moral crusade that promised to make the world "safe for democracy." His belief in the capability of all for self-government, linked with the explosive appeal of self-determination, had an impact with nationalist groups everywhere and made them look to the United States for the consummation of their desires. It is no exaggeration to state that, in the eyes of tens of millions the world over, here was a veritable Moses waiting, wanting to lead his children to the promised land. Wilson's oratory savored of the missionary spirit, and like all great preachers he could fire imaginations, kindle emotions, and lead people into battle for goals created often as much in their minds by their own hopes as by Wilson's words. And finally, in a world crisis, Wilson seemed to stand for all the best ideals of western civilization.

There were disadvantages as well. Moses himself, after all, did not get into the promised land but was buried in sight of it because of his arrogance and pride. It is astounding how often Wilson acted, as in Mexico and Russia, on the basis of an utter lack of knowledge of what was happening; nothing seemed to support his feeling of righteousness as did scanty information. The fact that neither the Mexican peasant nor the Russian peasant was prepared to handle the complex problems of creating and sustaining a democracy bothered Wilson not a whit. His belief in the perfectability of humankind caused Wilson to make some mistaken appraisals and to devise unworkable solutions. He seemed far more concerned with the purity of his motivations than he was with the nature of the regimes that he was called upon to deal with. Wilson's papers show surprisingly little study given to major policy decisions, for the president assumed he knew not only what was right but, more important to a president, what was wanted by the American people.

It was almost impossible to disagree with Wilson's broad principles which supported freedom, democracy, and justice; it was also much more difficult to define those terms when it came time to negotiate. Freedom for whom? Democracy for whom? Justice for whom? Each individual or group envisioned itself profiting, not anyone else; but when the final reckoning came, so did disillusionment, for in an intractable and complex world not all promises, explicit or implicit, could be kept to all groups.

Central America in the first decades of the twentieth century was a good example of the strengths and dangers of activist, interventionist policies. American interest in the Caribbean basin, centering around Panama, Santo Domingo, Haiti, Nicaragua, Venezuela, and Cuba, largely revolved around the security of the Panama Canal. Behind the specific goal stood a strong feeling that no foreign power should be allowed to acquire a strategic position anywhere, not only in the Caribbean, but in the Western Hemisphere. American economic investments, except in Cuba, were not large; most of the area simply did not look promising for economic development. Attempts to encourage political stability through encouragement of constitutionalism, support of fiscal responsibility, and the development of a political pluralism designed to lessen the domination of the military, thereby forestalling foreign attempts to take advantage of instability, worked on the international level but not on the domestic one. No foreign interventions actually took place, but the elites remained entrenched, the military grew in power, and the economic prospects of the middle and lower classes did not improve. Direct American intervention, despite good intentions, often led to counterproductive results that appeared to profit only those in power. Wilson hoped to change that pattern.

Premonitions of Wilson's conduct of American foreign relations in the period of the First World War are found in the often neglected Mexican crisis of 1913 to 1917. Mexico, in the old folk saying, "so far from God and so close to the United States," had suffered through a dictatorship from 1877 to 1912. In the latter year a revolution swept Porfirio Diaz from power. Francisco Madero, a revolutionary visionary, became the nominal head of the new Mexican government. Filled with good intentions but bereft of experience, Madero, like so many revolutionaries, was more talented in fomenting a change in government than he was in directing one once in power. He was not ruthless enough to establish an authoritarian regime nor supported by a broad and deep enough consensus to have a try at a stable democracy. With little sense of direction and stories of mystic seances in the presidential palace, it is little wonder that the coalition that had brought Madero to power began to fall to pieces. And it is also not surprising that the key element was the army. In a lightning coup in February 1913, Madero's army chief of staff, Victoriano Huerta, overthrew Madero. The hapless president died while he was on his way to prison. All of this was not an untypical story repeated many times in the kaleidoscopic rise and fall of Latin American governments. What was unusual, however, was the reaction of the United States government.

The events of 1912 and early 1913 had occurred during the last months of the lame duck William Howard Taft administration. Taft, cautious as always, had not extended diplomatic recognition to the Huerta government and obviously preferred to drop that hot potato in the lap of the new Wilson administration. But Wilson and his secretary of state, William Jennings Bryan, took an unprecedented position toward the new Huerta government. The president declared that he would not recognize the "government of a butcher." With high professorial ambitions he announced that he was going to "teach Latin Americans to elect good governments!" Bryan, through the Department of State, announced that it would henceforth be the policy of the United States government not to give *de facto* recognition to any government coming into power through violent, nondemocratic means. Selective and tentative at this point, for it was not applied to the Yuan Shih-K'ai government that had come into power in a similar pattern in China, this principle was to have a troublesome legacy not only in 1913 but in later decades when the United States did not recognize Bolshevik Russia or Communist China.

From the time of the first secretary of state, Thomas Jefferson, in 1789, to 1913, the United States had in almost all cases recognized *de facto* any regime that controlled the government of a country. If the government fulfilled its international obligations and behaved in what was viewed as a responsible manner, it was then given full *de jure* recognition. In Jefferson's view a government either existed or it did not. He did not inquire into how it had come into power, what type of government it was, or what its future intentions were. Realistic in approach, for these were internal conditions over which the United States had little if any control, Jefferson's policy welcomed all functioning governments into the international community; no one was to be left outside as a moral outcast. The act of recognition implied neither approval nor disapproval. On the surface it meant that the United States was dealing only with the reality of the existence of the government. Recognition did imply, however, that a recalcitrant or difficult government could be better dealt with, and perhaps influenced to change its ways, within the community rather than branded an outlaw and left unaffected by even the most elementary rules of international conduct. Wilson's new policy was an indication that he believed certain govern-

Woodrow Wilson and President William Howard Taft at the White House, 1913.

ments did not have high enough standards to belong to the international community.

Wilson's approach also opened a veritable Pandora's box which indeed left little except hope as a policy. Nonrecognition expressed, at the least, political and probably moral disapproval. Most large countries could live with such approbation, but small countries, particularly in Latin America, would find it difficult to have no political or economic relations with the Colossus of the North. Nonrecognition was clearly an interference in the domestic affairs of another country, and an open, if well intentioned, departure from the certain tradition of the nineteenth century. Nonrecognition would certainly encourage opposition groups within a nation to continue their activities. Would not the United States sooner or later have to support those groups with more than words?

How does one pick a group that is both "acceptable" and a "winner" out of a complex and unclear situation? Would not a continuation of the policy invite further revolution and bloodshed? What then would the logic of Wilson's position require? The degree of moral arrogance involved in judging the propriety and quality of another country's government was enormous and not guaranteed to win friends let alone influence potential enemies.

Finally, to compound the difficulties, Wilson withdrew the American ambassador, and with him one of the major reasons for having an embassy in a foreign nation—the collection of information. Wilson thus was operating with a high degree of ignorance. The president seemed more concerned with the purity of his motivations—the bringing of democracy to Mexico—than he was with the reality of the situation. Wilson's goal appeared unassailable; it was the means he chose to reach the goal with which reasonable men differed. When his intuitive sense ran into hard facts, it was difficult for him to back off and accept another solution.

Wilson did not care for situations that he could not control, and, like most activist presidents so admired by historians, he was certain that he had to do something, anything; he just could not leave Mexico alone. He tried through a special emmisary to get Huerta to hold an election in which he would not stand as a candidate; Huerta, not being stupid, refused to preside over his own demise. Wilson then attempted to pressure him politically and militarily by forbidding arms shipments to Huerta but allowing them to his main opponents, Venustiano Carranza and Pancho Villa, in the civil war still raging in Mexico.

With neither political nor economic solutions working, Wilson slowly but surely followed a path that led to the use of force. The petty Tampico incident of April 1915 offered the first opportunity. Eight American sailors from an American ship were accidentally arrested when they stumbled into a war zone in the Mexican port. They were almost immediately released, but the American commander, Admiral Henry T. Mayo, was furious, and he delivered an ultimatum to the Mexicans that they "publically hoist the American flag in a prominent position on shore and all salute it with twenty-one guns" as an apology. Mayo promised to fire a return salute. The president chose to back Mayo and on April

15 told leading congressmen that unless the Mexican government complied with his demands he would, with the approval of Congress which immediately passed a House resolution, impose a blockade and occupy Tampico.

Then word reached Washington that a German ship was on its way to Veracruz with a cargo of arms for Huerta. At 2:30 in the morning, the president, advised by the secretary of state in the famous "pajama conference," ordered the U.S. Navy to "Take Veracruz at once." On the morning of April 21, 1915, American troops landed and occupied a city that had been the opening wedge for invaders of Mexico from Cortez to the invasion of the American army during the Mexican War of 1848. The German ship, incidentally, detained and released, landed its arms for Huerta elsewhere. Still, by any reasonable definition, the United States in April 1915 had committed acts of war in Mexico.

Calmer heads then prevailed, and while an ABC (Argentina, Brazil, Chile) mediation was taking place, Huerta lost out in the civil war and abandoned his position. Carranza became president. In a quandary because Carranza had also ascended by undemocratic means, Wilson temporarily threw his support behind Pancho Villa when the latter promised to establish a constitutional government if he came to power. But Carranza inflicted a series of stunning defeats on Villa, and Wilson had made the mistake of picking a loser. Wilson recognized Carranza *de facto* on October 19, 1915. His troubles, however, had not ended since Villa decided to break up this new found romance by removing from a train seventeen young American engineering graduates on their way to new jobs in Mexican mines; Villa's forces executed sixteen of them on the spot. The Wilson administration did absolutely nothing. Villa then raided across the American border into Colombus, New Mexico, burned the town, and killed nineteen Americans in the process.

Twelve thousand American troops under General John J. Pershing were ordered into Mexico to find and punish Villa; the legal basis, admittedly weak, was an agreement with Carranza's ambassador permitting either country to enter the other country in the "hot pursuit" of bandits. Two or three border guards or rangers, however, were on a different scale than an entire army. Of course, it proved impossible to find Villa, who was hidden by Mexicans as a matter of national pride.

Carranza demanded the withdrawal of American troops after several weeks, and the possibility of armed clashes with Federal Mexican troops grew. It is remarkable that more incidents did not happen than actually occurred. On June 21, 1916, twelve of Pershing's men were killed and twenty-three captured as the United States and Mexico approached war once again.

Fortunately both sides backed off. The European crisis was increasing the possibility of an American involvement, Republicans were becoming more critical, and it was a election year; few American presidents want to run on a slogan of "he took us into war." A truce ensued and a commission discussed the crisis. On January 18, 1917, with the German crisis approaching a peak (the United States broke diplomatic relations with Germany two weeks later), Wilson withdrew Pershing from Mexico, and on March 13, 1917, Wilson granted *de jure* recognition to Carranza. The Mexican imbroglio was over, but the consequent ill feelings continued to poison relations between the two countries for years to come.

A situation developed in which Wilson had an honorable intention: to help bring democracy to Mexico. But the practical application of such a policy proved difficult and led the United States to the brink of war. Wilson's idealism and belief in the American mission of bringing democracy to others involved him in a complex situation that was difficult, if not impossible, to influence directly by either words or effective force. He might better have heeded the words of John Quincy Adams written in 1821:

> Whenever the standard [of freedom and independence] has been or shall be unfurled, there will her [America's] heart, her benediction, and her prayers be. But she goes not abroad in search of monsters to destroy. She is the well-wisher to the freedom and independence of all. She is the champion and vindicator only of her own. . . . She well knows that by once enlisting under other banners than her own, were they even the banners of foreign independence, she would involve herself beyond the power of extrication, in all the wars of interest and intrigue, of individual avarice, envy and ambition, which assume the colors and usurp the standard of freedom.

But it was the First World War, the Great War, from 1914 to 1918, that brought Wilson to an international stage and gave him the opportunity to present his ideas to a larger audience. When the "Guns of August" began to sound during the summer of 1914, their thunder came as a great surprise to many Americans. When President Wilson issued a proclamation of neutrality on August 4, 1914, and two weeks later urged Americans to be impartial in thought as well as in deed, his actions received strong public support. After all, the war was in Europe, and the United States did not seem to have a vital stake in its outcome. Few objected when Wilson neglected to send even a moral protest when Belgium's neutrality was brutally violated by Germany. The great majority of the American people did their best to follow the president's suggestion, but as time went on this course of action became harder and harder; in April 1917 the United States intervened in the war. What were the reasons for this seeming reversal of American neutrality? Why did the United States enter the First World War on the side of the Allies? Why did Wilson take his nation to war?

Some historians have suggested that the United States was taken in by the clever British propaganda that played on the close cultural ties between the two Anglo-Saxon nations and convinced Americans of the wickedness of Germany. There is little truth to this charge. First, there were Americans who did know what was going on in the world, and the remaining Americans were neither as naive nor as innocent as pictured. Second, the Germans themselves skillfully presented their case to the American public. Third, the famous atrocity stories about German actions, as circulated in the Bryce report, seemed to have little influence except on groups already pro-Allied. Fourth, it appears that American opinion was more affected by certain obvious facts, such as the taking of American lives by German submarines. Fifth, the factor that the majority of Americans were probably pro-Allied did not mean that they wanted to enter the war; it was possible to display sympathy but still remain neutral. And there was a sizable group of Americans who were either indifferent or even pronounced "a plague on both your houses," seeing no virtue in either the Allied or the Central Powers.

More important than the propaganda factor was the question of economic ties with the belligerents. The immediate result of the war was a financial panic on Wall Street, but by 1915 a vigorous boom set in. Belligerents on both sides hoped to buy materials in the United States. "Yes," a midwestern farmer said, "this war over in Europe is certainly a terrible thing. How high do you suppose the price of wheat will be by Christmas?" The United States from August 1914 to April 1917 sold approximately $6 billion worth of goods to the Allies; this was an increase in trade to the Allies from $825 million a year to $3.25 billion. Many Americans would like to have sold as much to the Central Powers, but because of the effectiveness of the British blockade, trade with Germany and Austria declined from $169.25 million in 1914 to $1.16 million in 1916. To Wilson, who argued that he was simply following traditional American neutrality practices, it was not the fault of the United States that the Allies could obtain food and supplies (in theory no contraband goods such as arms and ammunition) and the Central Powers could not. Under international law the United States had a perfect right to sell to both powers.

American actions, moreover, created problems as the amount of Allied purchases mounted. The Allies ran out of cash and would soon have to pay for goods in something other than cash. Normally, American bankers would have extended credit to them, but Secretary of State William Jennings Bryan, an authentic voice of rural populism, had placed a ban on loans because he believed money "the worst of all contrabands because it commands everything else." But in 1915, over the protests of Bryan, the Wilson administration reversed its policy; the Allies got money as well as supplies. President Raymond Poincaire of France remarked after this action that the United States had become an ally even though he did not expect the Americans to intervene until they had made more profits.

There is no question that the American economic stake in an Allied victory was great, and Wilson certainly recognized this. It is also true that the United States changed from a debtor to a creditor nation from 1914 to 1919. To suggest, however, as many isolationists did in the 1930s, that economic consideration was the key, even only, factor that took the United States into the war ignores the central role in that decision by Wilson. The president had built his entire political career on suspicion of and opposition to special economic interests; he seldom permitted

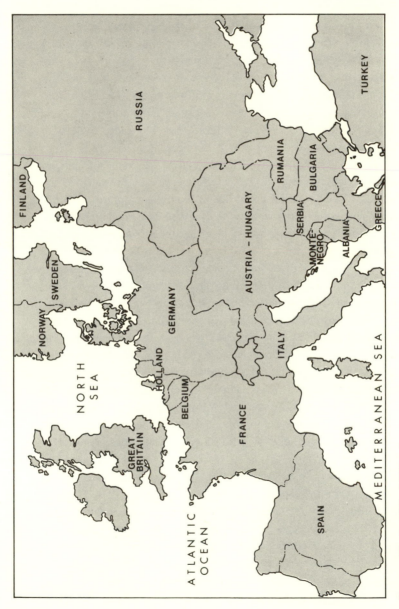

Europe During World War I

any group, including his closest advisers, let alone munitions manu-facturers, to dictate his politics. Control of events is a very crucial aspect in understanding Wilson's approach. Suffice it to say that while the president was certainly aware of economic considerations and would do nothing to destroy American prosperity, there is nothing in the record to indicate that he thought primarily in economic terms or that he allowed such considerations to influence his approach to neutral rights. Wilson was thinking largely on a moral and legal level, not on an economic or even a consistent political one.

Neither British propaganda nor close cultural ties with the Allies nor economic considerations caused him to focus on foreign affairs and finally call for American entrance into the war. The struggle over neutral rights and freedom of the seas led him step-by-step toward a bigger question: how best could both he and his country serve the cause of humanity in bringing the war to an end? More important, how could he guide, by forcing the belligerents to turn to the United States, the process into channels he could control that would result in a solution mirroring his progressive, idealist, rational approach? To ignore these considerations is to miss the entire essence of Wilson's missionary diplomacy.

Because of British control of the seas there were at first more com-plaints about British infringements of neutral rights and international law than there were about German violations. Great Britain, controlling the sea as it had for over one hundred years, was attempting, as it had with Napoleon, to prevent valuable materials or profitable trade from reaching the Central Powers. Britain, of course, presented a strict inter-pretation of neutral rights which clashed with the traditionally looser American interpretation. A reenactment of the War of 1812 was an initial possibility. It was the genius of careful British diplomacy, coupled with the emergence of German submarine warfare and the reluctance and tardiness of Wilson in challenging the British system, that prevented such a possibility.

The crucial period with regard to the British was from August 1914 to May 1915. Britain immediately mined the North Sea and began to impose a tight blockade upon Europe. The United States did not make a serious protest against the blockade until after it had been in effect almost six months. In this period no real thought was given to its implications. The result of the decision to accept the British maritime system was the same as if the United States had decided to impose its own blockade on the Central Powers. Some have suggested that an American embargo on British goods, such as that put into force in 1807 by Thomas Jefferson, might have influenced the British to lift many of their restrictions. But at no time in this period did the United States demand serious modification of the blockade or reinforce its complaints with threats of retaliation; the perfect opportunity for such steps was in this early period.

A stimulating book by historian John W. Coogan presents a substantial argument that Anglophiles in the Wilson administration conceded far more to Great Britain's initial maritime policy than London expected and further did so with the president's approval. Coogan concludes Wilson was not neutral, had no intention of being neutral, and had he truly been neutral the deadlocked belligerents might have eventually turned to him for mediation. Although Coogan makes a compelling case, Wilson publicly proclaimed that Britain's violations of international law were of a technical nature, open to settlement at the end of the war in a legal manner; Germany's transgressions with submarines, however, were "violations of the rights of humanity," even though the Allied blockade was to lead to severe hardships for German civilians. Wilson appeared to believe that the British would voluntarily mend their ways if he could only show them the right path. But once the British blockade was set up and operating, it was difficult to break simply by words. Then the British took other steps. They increased the number of items on the contraband list, and this resulted in the seizure of more and more American goods by the British. The American owners generally received compensation for such confiscated cargo. The only serious strain came over the British decision to seize cotton; this was close to home, for that was the main crop of the Democratic Solid South, Wilson's major domestic political support. The British averted a crisis in August 1916 when they agreed to purchase the American cotton crop before declaring it contraband. The British published a blacklist of American firms doing business with the Germans, opened American mail to the continent, and delayed American ships in British ports. Further, the British navy on occasion used the American flag, as in August 1916 when a German submarine stopped a British merchant ship and conducted a legal visit and search process. An American ship steamed up, filled with apparently curious Americans; when close enough, it lowered the American flag, raised the British flag, and blew the submarine out of the water. Expressions of joy did not characterize the German response to such incidents, but American resentment against British acts was more of a feeling than it was ever an organized movement articulated by the United States government.

The most important factor that turned American opinion against Germany was the submarine. By early 1915 the British had mined the North Sea and were beginning to enforce a tight naval blockade (although one was never actually declared) on Germany and neutral Europe. In order to break the blockade the Germans announced a submarine blockade of the British isles. In February 1915 the Germans had only 9 diesel submarines capable of reaching beyond Britain into the North Atlantic, and 12 gas-powered ones which could cover just the British Channel for a total of only 21 submarines. All enemy ships in the war zone risked destruction without warning, and neutrals received warning that they traveled at their own risk since Great Britain, the Germans charged, often used neutral flags to cover her own ships.

The Germans had picked a two-edged weapon—it was the only weapon with which they might stop the flow of materials to the Allies, but it was also the only method by which Germany could directly touch American interests. Wilson replied that the United States would hold Germany to a strict accountability for American ships and lives. He believed that Americans had a perfect right to the freedom of the seas and that German submarines must conform to the old rules of cruiser warfare as laid down under international law. Under these rules the submarine had to give warning to a merchant ship and see that passengers and crew disembarked before sinking the vessel. In this instance Wilson was attempting to enforce outmoded rules and was ignoring the practical realities facing the German submarine captains. A surfaced submarine was vulnerable to ramming or shelling by an armed merchant ship; also the submarine, small in size, could not possibly take on the crew and passengers of a vessel it was about to sink. To Wilson, however, the new weapon and its problems did not excuse its use by the Germans.

On May 7, 1915, the British liner *Lusitania* was sunk off the coast of Ireland with the loss of 1,198 lives, of which 128 were American; on board were also 4,200 cases of ammunition. American opinion displayed outrage, but few wanted war, and most agreed with Wilson, somewhat lost in his own words, when he said, "There is such a thing as a nation being so right that it does not need to convince others by force." Wilson insisted that Americans had a perfect right under international law to travel on any ships; Wilson and his Department of State adviser, Robert Lansing, were interpreting international law in their own way. It was true that a person on a belligerent vessel that was attacked had legal redress to the nation which owned the ship, but Wilson turned it around and said that a citizen had to look to his own government for protection of that right. Wilson wrote three notes to the Germans concerning the *Lusitania*. In the first note he demanded an end to all submarine warfare; the second note was so vigorous that Bryan thought it was unneutral and resigned as secretary of state rather than sign it; the third note, however, seemed to admit that submarine warfare was legal if conducted under cruiser warfare rules as much as possible. The Germans were slow to reply, but in February 1916 they did express regret for the sinking and promised to pay an indemnity but would not admit that it was an illegal act. Since Wilson had backed down somewhat in his notes, there were Germans who concluded that in the long run he would protest but do nothing. After the sinking of another British liner, the *Arabic* on August 19, 1915, with the loss of two American lives, the German ambassador in Washington gave the so-called *Arabic* pledge that German submarines would not sink unarmed passenger liners unless they attempted to run. This soothed Americans as well as Wilson's sense of honor, and the first phase of German submarine warfare came to an end. It appeared to be a diplomatic triumph for Wilson.

There are two interesting facts that should be borne in mind. First, Americans had 5,427,636 tons of ships registered out of a world total of 45 million; but 4,703,000 tons of those American ships operated on the Great Lakes. This meant that most American goods and people traveled to and from Europe on non-American ships. Second, of the approximately 250 Americans who died as a result of submarine attacks prior to breaking of diplomatic relations in February 1917, only three were on board American ships. Thus a small number of Americans, who knowingly and willingly sailed into a war zone, were by their choice putting themselves and their country at risk. One could well ask if it were a responsibility on the part of the Wilson administration to support their acts. President Franklin Roosevelt, facing a somewhat similar situation in 1939, gave a clear cut "no" to that question.

By 1916 Germany had forty-seven submarines and began the second phase of submarine warfare on February 10 of that year when it announced that it would sink all armed merchant ships without warning beginning March 1. Wilson protested without success. Congress tried to pass the Gore-McLemore resolution that warned Americans against traveling on belligerent ships, but Wilson successfully defeated the measure and continued to argue that if the government backed down on its stand, the whole fabric of international law and justice would go up in flames. On March 24, 1916, the Germans sank the British passenger liner *Sussex,* with the injury of several Americans in what appeared to be a deliberate violation of the *Arabic* pledge. Wilson came before Congress in April and read a note he had sent to Berlin. If the Germans did not stop sinking armed and unarmed merchant ships and passenger vessels, the United States would sever diplomatic relations with Germany.

Unknown to Wilson, his message brought to a boil the controversy between the military lords of Germany, Generals Paul von Hindenburg and Erich Ludendorff, and Imperial Chancellor Theobald von Bethmann Hollweg. The Foreign Office in particular felt the risk was too great; it did not want to provoke the United States into the war at that time. Its viewpoint, for the last time, won out over the military and on May 4, Germany, in the so-called *Sussex* pledge, agreed to observe the rules of visit and search before sinking a merchant ship. It warned the United States, however, that Germany might adopt a different attitude if the United States did not force Great Britain to follow international law as well. Wilson replied that Germany had to respect neutral rights even if the other belligerents did not, since the responsibility in such cases was single and not joint. But the next incident would force Wilson to break diplomatic relations. He had put the initiative in the hands of the Germans and left himself little room for maneuver.

Wilson's success appeared so great that his followers used the slogan "he kept us out of war" in the presidental campaign of 1916. In a very close and important election Wilson barely defeated the Republican candidate, Charles Evans Hughes. How Hughes would have handled the problems that Wilson was to face in the future, of course, we will never know, but Hughes later became a most able secretary of state, and it is possible that he might have handled the developing problems in a more realistic manner.

In 1914 when the armies of Europe marched to war, the military forces of the United States totaled 165,919 men (98,544 in the army; 56,989 in the navy; and 10,386 in the marines); by 1916 the total had increased only slightly to 179,376. When in October 1914 Representative Augustus P. Garner, not incidentally Henry Cabot Lodge's son-in-law, called for a commission to examine the status of American military forces, President Wilson replied that the United States would continue to rely on volunteers in the event of a threat but that he saw no danger at that time. As the war in Europe deepened, pressure groups began to form, both within and outside the government, calling for preparedness; in particular, the Progressive Republicans led by former President Theodore Roosevelt called for greater defense expenditures. Unwilling to let political opponents seize the leadership of the movement with a presidential election in the offing in 1916, Wilson in 1915 came out for moderate increases. He also said, however, that the American navy, still viewed as preeminently a defensive force, should become the equal of any other navy in the world; that stance led to a large naval construction bill in 1916. Wilson, although pushed by Secretary of War Lindley M. Garrison, remained cautious on the army. It was not until early 1916, while on a political speaking tour, that Wilson publicly put himself at the head of a program for increased defense spending, still indicating, however, that he saw no threat necessitating large expenditures. Garrison, wanting just that, resigned, and Wilson, abdicating leadership in the preparedness movement, dumped the program in the lap of Congress. In stealing the preparedness issue from the Republicans he almost moderated it into uselessness. When the U.S. went to war in 1917, it took considerable time to mobilize and bring its power to bear. Except in the Mexican imbroglio, Wilson demonstrated that he saw little connection between the threat of military force and a strong diplomatic negotiating stance.

One of the major objectives of Wilson's neutrality was to fulfill the requirements of mediation. Neither he nor the American people seemed to have believed that American national security was at stake; therefore Wilson could afford not to take sides. As historian William Langer has written, Wilson knew very "little and evidently cared less about the origins and causes of the cataclysm." But he apparently thought that hateful though the war was, it might provide an opportunity for him and his country through mediation to serve the greater cause of humanity. Wilson saw no difference between the two warring groups and said in December 1916 that "the objects which the statesman of the belligerents of both sides have in mind in this war are virtually the same. . . ." With this view of the war Wilson concluded that a mediation could perhaps bring about a situation in which a new international order might be set up with the United States as one of its leaders.

A private, nonadministration attempt to end the war briefly grabbed headlines. On December 4, 1915, the *Oscar II* sailed with 140 (63 delegates and 57 reporters among the group) persons on the Henry Ford "peaceship." Ford, in an idealistic, pacific effort "to get the boys out of the trenches before Christmas," had chartered the ship. From the very first it was an ill-fated venture: "the illustrious scrambled to avoid being caught among the peace ship's passengers," and there were jokes such as "They stopped building flivvers the day the peace ship sailed, because they ran out of nuts." The sincerity of those who sailed was clear. But Ford himself, after the ship got to Norway, came right back and the members were left to approach the warring powers by themselves. The entire episode did more harm than good and made Americans look ridiculous, at least to themselves.

Colonel Edward House, Wilson's closest adviser, was then sent to Europe; he made little progress in Paris and Berlin but he did have a long conversation with the British foreign minister, Sir Edward Grey, in February 1916. Grey saw he could best approach the Wilson administration through the question of freedom of the seas. Grey said that Great Britain and the United States, along with all the other nations in the world, should get together and guarantee freedom of the seas for all vessels in wartime or otherwise; any breaking of the agreement would then be met by a combination of all nations against the aggressor. What Grey was really suggesting was then nothing less than collective security against potential aggression by way of the traditional American interest in freedom of the seas. Grey and House talked further and the final result was the famous House-Grey memorandum. It provided that the United States, on hearing from France and Great Britain that they desired mediation, would call a conference. "Should the Allies accept this proposal, and should Germany refuse it, the United States would probably enter the war against Germany . . . and if such conference failed to secure peace the United States would probably leave the conference as a belligerent on the side of the Allies." Wilson added the "probably" each time. Whether he did this primarily because he desired to keep the United States out of the war or because he recognized the constitutional limitations on such a promise is unclear. Critics of Wilson contend that the House-Grey memorandum proves that Wilson intended all along to intervene in the war on the side of the Allies—thus that Wilson was really not neutral.

The British, who were as much opposed to American mediation as ever, were not called upon for any commitment; indeed the whole scheme was not to go into operation until the British asked for its implementation. It was a very favorable offer which the British never took advantage of, perhaps because they were not sure that Congress would actually vote for war and let Wilson keep his bargain. Britain did not want mediation because it thought it could defeat Germany and dictate terms of peace to Germany far more favorable to Great Britain than Wilson would ever secure in any mediation; and certainly Germany felt the same way. Arthur S. Link, who has completed five volumes of his definitive study on Wilson, concludes that the House-Grey memorandum was a movement by Wilson to keep the United States out of the war by mediation. The argument continues, but certainly nothing came of the memorandum.

During the summer of 1916 Wilson decided the British would never ask for or accept American mediation as long as the Allies had any hope of winning the war; Grey made it plain that any mediation would be regarded by the Allies as a hostile act designed to deprive them of their chance of victory. There is some evidence that the British decision to prolong the war, and by 1916 most of the members of the British cabinet were not displaying any concern for the interests and feelings of the United States, was based on a belief that sooner or later Germany would break the *Sussex* pledge. Wilson's response to this rebuff was to strengthen American neutrality and to press forward on his own independent campaign for peace. He asked for and received from Congress the power to deny the use of American ports to ships of any nation that discriminated against American commerce. This, of course, would work most effectively against the British. Wilson did not move quickly enough on his second step because the German government, stalling for time, announced on December 12, 1916, that it was willing to enter a peace conference. On December 18 the president then asked the belligerents to state their war aims. To Wilson, America was now entering the crucial stage.

The British stated privately to Wilson on January 10, 1917, that they were willing to come to a peace conference; the reason for this sudden and surprising reversal is unknown because the British records for this period are incomplete. Some ground exists, however, for the belief that the British, knowing the Germans were about to begin unrestricted submarine warfare again, were simply buying Wilson's good will. If so, it was a shrewd move. The president, not waiting for the German declaration of war aims, on January 22, 1917, outlined the kind of peace he expected. Wilson called for a peace among equals, a "peace without victory," without annexations or indemnities or vengeance. Wilson was sure he could force the British into a peace conference, by economic pressure if necessary. The decision for war or peace would then reside in the hands of the Germans.

When the war began in 1914 the German government had not formed any clear objective as to what it expected out of the war, but as the years went by the Germans decided that they must gain something out of the bloody struggle. Their maximum demands included the establishment of a Polish kingdom under German control, German annexation of Lithuania and Courland, destruction of British naval supremacy, an indemnity from Britain and France, the annexation of Belgium and parts of France, and the annexation of the Belgian Congo. Even a partial realization of these demands would have secured German domination of Europe. The Germans realized that Wilson would never support such demands. As a consequence, historians can safely conclude that no German leader ever seriously considered accepting Wilson's mediation. They would use Wilson as a pawn to get the British to a conference, but they would accept his mediation only after a preliminary negotiation had already settled everything of importance.

The Germans, recognizing that they could never win their goals by diplomacy, decided to begin their third and last submarine campaign; they now had over one hundred submarines available. On January 31, 1917, they informed Wilson that on February 1 they would sink on sight all ships within a stipulated war zone around Britain and in the eastern Mediterranean. This was a fateful decision—one of the most important ever made by Germany. The military men had convinced the German government that they now had sufficient submarines to bring Britain to the verge of starvation within five months. They realized that this might mean war with the United States, but they believed that American participation would make little or no difference. The German political leaders, as German historian Fritz Fischer has made so clear, must share the blame for this decision. Had the Germans decided to sink only belligerent ships, exclusive of larger liners, and spared American ships, there is a great possibility that the United States would not have entered the war. This limited objective never entered the heads of the Germans, and with the collapse of Russia it might well have worked.

Wilson had no alternative but to break diplomatic relations on February 3, 1917; even then he announced a period of watchful waiting. He seemed to say that if they spared American lives and American ships, he would do nothing. If the Germans attacked American ships, he would defend them by armed neutrality. This was not the language of war, and in March 1917 it appeared that Wilson had made his decision in favor of a limited defensive war on the seas. What caused him to abandon his policy?

Several considerations weighed upon Wilson in the period from February 3 to the declaration of war on April 4. First, it was clear that the Germans intended to carry out their threat. They sank a British liner, the *Laconia,* and three American merchant ships. The possibility of an armed neutrality was considered and abandoned not only because of its difficulties of operation but, perhaps more importantly, because an armed neutral firing at both sides would make mediation difficult. Armed neutrality would not allow Wilson to control the situation for a mediation.

Second, that strange document known as the Zimmermann telegram had an impact. A message from the German foreign secretary, Alfred Zimmermann, to the German embassy in Mexico City through a relay in Washington, D.C., offered Mexico, should war occur, and should Mexico join Germany, and should Germany win, the return of the American Southwest lost in 1848. The same message also announced the unrestricted submarine warfare campaign. It was sent by the Germans on the American cable in code, the British having cut the German cable in 1914. The message was picked up by the British who were, unknown to the Americans, tapping the American cable. In January 1917 the British knew they had a bombshell but could not tell the Americans how they had gotten it, nor did they want the Germans to know they had broken their code. Practicing the old diplomatic rule of neither telling a lie nor telling the whole truth, they finally passed the message on to the Americans. Its release convinced many Americans that Germany was not an illusionary threat to the United States but a real one.

Wilson's cabinet favored war. It is difficult, if not impossible, to determine what public opinion favored, but Wilson read it as at least permitting war. On April 2 he asked for a war resolution and said Americans would fight "for democracy, for the right of those who submit to authority to have a voice in their own governments, for the rights and liberties of small nations, for a universal dominion of right by such a concert of free peoples as shall bring peace and safety to all nations and make the world itself at last free." With these ringing words in its ears Congress by a count of 82-6 in the Senate on April 4 and 373-50 in the House on April 6 voted for war.

Why did the United States ultimately enter the First World War? There are conflicting answers. One is that Wilson consciously or unconsciously took the United States in to prevent Germany from winning and thus upsetting an existing balance of power that favored the United States. Another answer is that Americans blundered into war due to a combination of mistakes, pro-Allied sentiment, and greed. Still another answer is that it was inevitable and that nothing Wilson did or could have done would have changed the decision. Arthur Link, the premier Wilson scholar of his generation, has written that:

> He [Wilson] was not influenced by considerations of immediate national security. That is, he did not accept belligerency because he thought that the Allies were about to lose and a German victory would imperil American security. But Wilson was profoundly affected by considerations of the long-range interest. He stubbornly resisted the decision for war because he believed that American interests, to say nothing of the interests of mankind, would be best protected and served by a negotiated peace without victory. Wilson accepted belligerent status for two reasons, mainly: because he could see no other way to protect American national rights and shipping on the high seas in the face of repeated German assaults and because he believed that the war was in its final stages and American participation would hasten its end.

Still, however, is there not strong ground for another conclusion and perhaps a broader speculation?

First, is it not possible, as his whole mediation effort suggests, that Wilson saw a greater chance for him to control the outcome, to lead the peace into channels he could construct, as the leader of a belligerent power rather than as a neutral? Did he not think, like other statesmen before and since, that he could pursue good ends through bad means?

Second, a theme we shall return to in the next chapter, is it not also possible that the United States went into the war in the wrong manner, for the wrong reasons, and that the tragic outcome of the American effort both at Versailles and in the Senate, was in large part predicated on those mistaken initial steps?

Selected Reading

Arthur Link is the leading Wilson scholar of his generation. His monumental *The Papers of Woodrow Wilson* (1966–   ), is over fifty volumes and has now reached the year 1919. His uncompleted *Wilson* biography (1947–   ), has five volumes covering to 1917. Increasingly uncritical of Wilson, Link's works include two other important volumes: *Woodrow Wilson: Revolution, War, and Peace* (1979) and *The Higher Realism of Woodrow Wilson and Other Essays* (1971). Other works bearing the Link stamp of approval are John M. Mulder's *Woodrow Wilson: The Years of Preparation* (1978) and Edwin A. Weinstein's *Woodrow Wilson: A Medical and Psychological Biography* (1981).

More critical assessments would include Alexander and Juliette George, *Woodrow Wilson and Colonel House: A Personality Study* (1956), Arthur Walworth, *Woodrow Wilson* (1965), and an earlier Link, *Woodrow Wilson and the Progressive Era: 1910–1917* (1954). Otis L. Graham's *The Great Campaigns: Reform and War in America, 1900–1928* (1971) places the Wilson years in a domestic context.

U.S.-Mexican relations are well described in *The United States and Huerta* (1969) by Kenneth J. Grieb, *Diplomacy and Revolution: U.S.-Mexican Relations Under Wilson and Carranza* (1977) by Mark T. Gilderhus, *An Affair of Honor: Woodrow Wilson and the Occupation of Veracruz* (1962) by Robert Quirk, and *The Secret War in Mexico: Europe, the United States, and the Mexican Revolution* (1981) by Fredrick Katz. A good survey of Mexican history can be found in Ramon Eduardo Ruiz's *The Great Rebellion: Mexico, 1905–1924* (1980).

Ernest May in his *The World War and American Isolation, 1914–1917* (1959) agrees with Link that Wilson had no alternatives to the steps that took the United States into the war. In *Woodrow Wilson and the Balance of Power* (1955) Edward H. Buehrig argues for the realism of Wilson's motivations. *Too Proud to Fight: Woodrow Wilson's Neutrality* (1975) by Patrick Devlin concentrates on legal issues of neutrality and is critical of Wilson. John Coogan in his *The End of Neutrality: The United States, Britain, and Maritime Rights, 1899–1915* (1981) finds Wilson's actions pro-British and unneutral. Classic studies by Walter Millis, *The Road to War: America, 1914–1917* (1935) and Charles Seymour, *American Neutrality, 1914–1917: Essays on the Causes of American Intervention in the World War* (1935) remain worth reading.

More specialized works would include: Barbara Tuchman's *The Zimmermann Telegram* (1958), Charles DeBenedetti's *Origins of the Modern American Peace Movement, 1915–1929* (1978), Horace C. Peterson and Gilbert C. Fite's *Opponents of War, 1917–1918* (1957), and Thomas A. Bailey and Paul B. Ryan's *The Lusitania Disaster: An Episode in Modern Warfare and Diplomacy* (1975). *Politics of Frustration: The United States in German Naval Planning, 1889–1941* (1976) by Holger H. Herwig and *Germany's Aims in the First World War* (1967) by Fritz Fischer illuminate the German aspect of the controversy.

3   Peacemaking, 1918–1922

In Lord Tennyson's lyric poem Ulysses, the lost leader, on his way back home after the Trojan War, calls to his followers: "Come, my friends, / 'Tis not too late to seek a newer world. / For my purpose holds to sail beyond the sunset. . . ." In a twentieth-century prototype, Woodrow Wilson took up Ulysses' fallen standard and battled the gods just as valiantly. He too gambled with "fortunatus" to attempt a new world order, based on an ideological proposal of "self determination," and a League of Nations to make a world "safe" for democratic principles. While Ulysses faced Poseidon and Circe, Wilson's gods were just as unpredictable and complex; he defied the heads of government in Europe, the American public, and—most disastrously—the leadership of the United States Senate, to bring about his own personal vision of democracy and his own tragic finale. But in the spring of 1917 that was still in the future.

America went to war in that fateful spring with the usual increase in military forces, the mobilization of American industry, and a call to defeat the dastardly Huns. But Wilson from the very first, despite his oft-quoted talk with newspaperman Frank Cobb the night before the war declaration in which he expressed concern about what war might do to American values, was primarily interested not so much in waging the war but in bringing it to a satisfactory conclusion. The president, moreover, wanted to conclude the war in such a way that he would be able to control events so that his principles would form the foundation of the peace treaty.

The entrance of the United States into the war to make "the world safe for democracy," however appealing and fine sounding, was a goal beyond the capacity and reach of American power. When it became clear that most governments in the world, as always, would remain nondemocratic and that even the existing democracies struggled for survival, disillusionment set in. This contributed heavily to an interwar isolationist mood in the United States that had as one of its tenets the belief that the American government should not have gone into the First World War. But what if the Wilson administration had entered the war not for an unreachable goal but for one that was within the parameters of American power? Had the United States entered the war on a much narrower basis—predicated on a realistic appraisal of the national interest, such as not allowing Germany to upset a balance of power that had worked favorably for the United States—could not a limited peace treaty have been written protecting that narrow interest and combining a destruction of German power with her restoration to the world community as a functioning member? Such a treaty would have passed the United States Senate and, as the aftermath of the Second World War demonstrated, was an achievable goal.

Enormous hysteria against the Germans, however, had built up as wartime propaganda developed images of Atilla the Hun stabling horses in churches and German soldiers impaling babies on their bayonets. A history professor at Indiana University wrote: "The Kaiser and his Potsdam gang made this war. As they appealed to the sword they shall perish by the sword. We can have no peace with the Hohenzollerns. We should demand an unconditional surrender of this barbarous power that has assaulted our civilization." Germans were cast outside the pale of civilization, and righteous but misguided patriots in America were allowed to carry out serious infringements on both truth and honor. There is, here, an important point.

Emotions that are whipped up in wartime against an enemy, especially the view that they are barbarians, no longer fit to belong to the human community of nations, make it extremely difficult to turn around immediately and write a reasonable peace that emphasizes restoration rather than punishment. Abraham Lincoln, some fifty years prior, saw the true test not in merely winning the war, but binding up the nation's wounds. He, unlike Wilson, saw that current enemies must be future partners if the war effort was to have any lasting meaning. Wilson should have attempted to restrain the hysteria and to have educated the American people about the meaning of his "peace without victory" theme. Most Americans probably wanted victory first and a way to end all wars second. A stronger and clearer stance by Wilson might have diminished his image as a war leader but also might have rallied greater public support for his peace plans. When he did attempt to explain, it was too late. This lack of public support and his failure to give the American people any real understanding of the way that he saw either the war or the peace was compounded by his dealings with Congress.

Wilson announced to Congress on January 8, 1918, his program for peace, which he summarized under the following Fourteen Points: 1) open convenants of peace, openly arrived at; 2) freedom of the seas; 3) removal "so far as possible" of economic barriers; 4) reduction of armaments "to the lowest point consistent with domestic safety;" 5) adjustment of colonial claims; 6) evacuation of Russia; 7) evacuation and restoration of Belgium; 8) return of Alsace-Lorraine to France; 9) readjustment of Italian frontiers "along clearly recognizable lines of nationality;" 10) "autonomous development" for all peoples of Austria-Hungary; 11) evacuation of Rumania, Serbia, and Montenegro, with access to the sea for Serbia; 12) reduction of Turkey to territory containing only peoples of Turkish descent; 13) independence of Poland, with access by Poland to the sea; and 14) establishment of a League of Nations. Wilson later added thirteen supplementary points to the original fourteen, but nearly all of them are restatements of principles implicit in the Fourteen Points (like self-determination). This was basically a statement of war aims which Wilson sprang on an unsuspecting Congress. He might have either talked to congressional leaders prior to the announcement of the program or attempted to get Congress to endorse it. He did neither.

Internationally the impact of the Fourteen Points was tremendous. It was a masterstroke of what is now called "ideological warfare." It undermined the willingness of the peoples of the Central Powers to continue the struggle. In calling for self-determination, Wilson aroused the hopes of oppressed peoples everywhere who desired autonomy, freedom, or nationhood.

The Allied nations, as one might suspect, were less than enthusiastic. They had their own war aims that long antedated those of the late arriving Americans. The American entrance into the war made the crucial difference. German submarine warfare had Great Britain in serious trouble, France was exhausted, and, more important, shortly after the Russian Revolution the Russians left the war, making it possible for the Germans to transfer Eastern Front troops to the Western Front. At best a stalemate loomed for the Allies.

When the United States entered the war, the Allies sent delegations across the Atlantic to secure American aid. The Wilson administration at that time might have bargained with the Allies about the series of secret treaties that they had signed with each other. Those treaties divided up most of the territory of the Central Powers; such a division was to take place at a peace conference, assuming the Allies won, of course. Wilson could have forced the Allies to abandon many of the harsh features of these treaties which did, in fact, become the basis of the Treaty of Versailles in 1919. Desperately in need of American aid, the Allies might have conceded much more to Wilsonian idealism in 1917 than in 1919 after the victory was won. To have bargained with the Allies at that critical time would have seemed harsh to many moralists, but it almost certainly would have worked. Wilson thus brought American power into the war without any guarantee of the application of his principles. Nevertheless, it was the United States which in effect postponed discussing the postwar settlement when Wilson chose to ignore the secret treaties. Also noteworthy is the fact that the United States entered the war as an "Associated" power, not as an "Allied" power; there was never an alliance between the Allies and the United States. Wilson often appeared to his fellow wartime collaborators more an arbiter than a member of the coalition. All of this meant that the Allies did not regard the Fourteen Points as carved in marble or as the final program for the peace conference.

At the beginning of October 1918 the German high command, realizing that American intervention in the war was proving more decisive than they had expected, advised the German government to seek an armistice. Expecting a softer peace from Wilson than from the Allies, they dickered with the president for almost a month. During that time

Kaiser Wilhelm abdicated and a German People's Government came into existence. While Wilson was negotiating with the Germans, Colonel House was talking to the Allies. France, Italy, and England accepted the Fourteen Points as the basis of peace with two reservations. On Wilson's second point, "freedom of the seas," Britain retained her freedom of action, and the Allies wanted the Central Powers to pay an indemnity for civilian damages.

Wilson accepted both and sent the news to the Germans. On November 11, 1918, in a railway car near Compiègne, the Germans signed the armistice agreement based on Wilson's Fourteen Points and "subsequent messages." This became a point of dispute after the signing of the Treaty of Versailles. Did the Allied and Associated Powers break the armistice agreement under which Germany surrendered by including other penalties not mentioned in the armistice in the Treaty of Versailles? Critics of the peace say "Yes"; supporters of the peace say "No." Apparently this was Wilson's hour of triumph, but even in November 1918 there were storm clouds on the horizon. At this time Wilson made several crucial decisions. First, he decided to go to the peace conference in Paris in person. One can argue that in so doing he lost contact with American opinion; that by remaining in the United States he would have retained control of the domestic situation. But on this debatable point one can also argue that the harshness of the Treaty of Versailles might have increased in severity if Wilson had not attended. After all, Wilson had more popularity in 1918 than almost any American president, before or since, has had. Wilson looked like the savior of the world in 1918, and those who today stress prestige might note that Wilson, armed with perhaps the greatest prestige an American president has ever had in the international arena, met tragic defeat both in Paris and at home.

Second, Wilson had made the political error of asking for a Democratic Congress in the mid-term election of November 1918 so that he might "continue to be your unembarrassed spokesman in affairs at home and abroad." In so doing he cast a bad reflection on the Republicans by implying that they had not supported him in the war effort. The voters elected Republican majorities in both houses of Congress; this gave the Republicans the right to organize Congress and made Henry Cabot Lodge the chairman of the Senate Foreign Relations Committee.

The end of the war, Buffalo, N.Y., 1919.

Wilson had said during the campaign that a Republican victory would be a "repudiation" of his leadership, and thus, in his own words, he stood repudiated before the world. His arch enemy, Theodore Roosevelt, wired the Allies that the American people had just repudiated their president. Wilson, a former history-government professor, might also have remembered that the presidential party in power almost always loses the mid-term election. It is ironic that Wilson, who often argued that the Allied leaders did not represent their people, should have ended up the one about whom questions were raised. This election caused a great deal of uneasiness in Paris since the Allies were not sure that Wilson really represented the United States and that America would keep the promises that Wilson was making.

Third, Wilson neglected to place any key Republican leaders or senators on the peace commission that he took to Europe with him. This was the gravest error of all and the most inexcusable. There was certainly reason for not taking Lodge, an old enemy, but what possible reason was there for not taking such distinguished Republicans as William Howard Taft, Charles Evans Hughes, or Elihu Root, all of whom favored the League of Nations idea? The Republican party was not isolationist and, in fact, had led the United States into world affairs during the 1890s and the time of Theodore Roosevelt; the defeat of the League was not clearly foreordained as the Republicans had been more favorable to international cooperation than the Democrats prior to 1914 and still were split as a result of the struggle for president in 1912. Wilson, some have suggested, was psychologically incapable of working with members of a political party who he believed opposed his plans out of pure personal spite and partisanship. It is all but impossible to understand Wilson not including senators on the peace commissions since the Senate would have to give its advice and consent to any treaty. The Senate was well known for the jealous guarding of its prerogative; to attempt to gain a segment of support for the treaty by having a senator on the peace commission seemed a practical consideration. It was one Wilson chose not to make.

After a triumphal tour of Europe where literally millions lined the streets to see Wilson and toast him as savior, the president went to Paris to negotiate the treaty. While it may seem an obvious point, it should be noted that Wilson was the representative of only one country, that other countries and other diplomats also had their ideas about the peace conference. If Wilson had not developed a carefully thought-out plan, others had. Representing France was its seventy-year-old premier, Georges Clemenceau, who viewed Wilson's program with some contempt and is reported to have said, "who is this Wilson with his fourteen points? God only has ten." His key assumption was that Germany must be kept down; he would accomplish this by French control of key points along the Rhine and by asking the United States and England to come to the aid of France in the event of future German agression. He viewed a league not as the only security but as additional security. Representing England was Prime Minister David Lloyd George, who had a somewhat crude legal mind and absolutely no knowledge of European geography. He wanted to prevent German domination of the continent, but he also wanted to prevent French domination. He favored a Germany strong enough to put some pressure on France and a Germany that would have enough money to buy British goods.

Wilson's greatest success came at the conference when he convinced the Allies that the treaty should include the League of Nations covenant or charter; he could not see the acceptance of one without the other. The League's most important responsibility was to preserve peace. On any controversy likely to lead to war, members agreed to submit either to arbitration or to the League council and not to go to war for at least three months after an award was made, a sort of cooling-off period; they also promised not to go to war against nations complying with the recommendations of the League. The council might recommend economic or military sanctions against nations resorting to war in violation of these pledges. Wilson considered that the key part of the covenant was Article 10, which read: "The members of the League undertake to respect and preserve as against external aggression the territorial integrity and existing political independence of all members of the League. In case of any such aggression or in case of any threat or danger of such aggression the Council shall devise upon the means by which the obligations shall be fulfilled."

One of Wilson's major problems was the secrecy at the conference. All sorts of rumors appeared in American newspapers, and opposition began to develop to the League. Much of the criticism was based upon pure ignorance since no one in the United States had actually seen the official draft; nothing apparently confirms one in his opinion more strongly than ignorance, as Wilson, who was from Princeton, found out when he returned for a short visit to the United States. He ran into the carping criticism of Lodge, a graduate of Harvard, who said, "As an English composition it does not rank high. It might get by at Princeton but certainly not at Harvard." Furthermore, Republican senators had no real idea of what was in the treaty but knew they were against it. Lodge presented the famous "Round Robin," a petition signed by thirty-nine Republican senators who announced that they could not agree to the League of Nations as it then stood. This was three more votes than the necessary one-third required to defeat a treaty. Wilson did agree to work for several amendments—members of the League could withdraw if they wished, the Monroe Doctrine was specifically approved, domestic questions were exempted from the jurisdiction of the League, and nations could refuse to accept mandates. There is little doubt that Wilson, in insisting on these amendments when he got back to Paris, weakened his moral position because he was asking for special privileges; there is just as little doubt that they were necessary if he hoped to get the treaty through the Senate. He would not modify Article 10.

On Wilson's return to Paris the diplomats got down to the serious business of completing the Treaty of Versailles. France wanted to detach the Rhineland and make it a French-dominated buffer state. Wilson prevented that, but the French did get Alsace-Lorraine back, control of the Saar Basin for fifteen years and a plebiscite at the end of that time, occupation of the Rhineland for fifteen years, and permanent demilitarization of both banks of the Rhine. The British and the Americans, however, had to sign a separate treaty promising aid to the French in case of German attack. Never ratified, it died in the American Senate Foreign Relations Committee in the struggle over the League.

On the issue of freedom of the seas, one of the main reasons for American entrance into the war, and a point on which the British had reserved freedom of action, nothing specific was included in the peace treaty.

On the impartial settlement of colonial claims, Wilson ran into the secret treaties by which the Allies had divided up the colonial areas. Wilson hoped to see these colonies go to the smaller powers, but under the mandate system he achieved a compromise in which the colonies went to the victorious Allies much as stipulated in the secret treaties. There was an element of League control in that the mandate powers had to submit annual reports on their activities.

It was on the question of territorial settlements that Wilson suffered some setbacks. He did succeed, however, in restricting the French, who wanted a great deal of German territory, and the Italians, who wanted Fiume. The principle of self-determination was followed, as one observer has pointed out, for friends of the Allies but not always for foes. For example, the conference gave Italy the South Tyrol (control of the Brenner Pass), which included 200,000 Austrian-Germans and forbade Austria to unite with Germany even though many Austrians desired such a step. Wilson also agreed to the Japanese occupation of the former German concessions in Shantung; because of this, China refused to sign the peace treaty and Wilson faced heavy criticism during the Senate debates. In spite of these failures, however, Wilson came as close to making an ethnological map of Europe as was possible. If one believes that states should be created on the idea of common race and language, there is little to quibble with in Wilson's program, since the success far offset the failures. But the break-up of the Austrian-Hungarian Empire on that basis, rather than on grounds of political viability and national strength, did not contribute to the future stability of Europe as the weaker successor states fell under the domination of stronger powers.

On the issue of reparations Wilson suffered his gravest defeat. The Wilson peace program had not envisioned harsh indemnities or reparations. In utter disregard of the armistice agreement, whereby Germany had agreed to pay only civilian damages, the British and French decided that Germany should shoulder, if possible, much of the cost of the war. That bill included pensions to disabled veterans, a German admission of responsibility for all war losses, the French to have the option of occupying the Rhineland if Germany did not pay her bill, the French to have the right to seize over $5 billion worth of German property, and French ownership of German coal mines in the Saar Valley. After the conference a commission finally presented Germany with a bill of

$33 billion. John M. Keynes in his *Economic Consequence of the Peace,* a fantastically popular book in 1920, argued beyond a doubt the utter absurdity of the reparations settlement. His conclusion was that Germany could not possibly pay such a sum. This book had a considerable effect on the great disillusionment about the treaty that developed in the interwar period. A later scholar, Étienne Mantoux, in his *The Carthaginian Peace, or the Economic Consequences of Mr. Keynes,* argued that the Keynes book encouraged the Germans not to pay the bill—which they did not. Others have pointed out that Hilter spent far more rearming Germany. The question, it seems, was not whether it was possible for the Germans to pay, but whether they were willing to do so. If the Allies intended to saddle them with the huge bill, they should have been willing to coerce Germany to pay.

The practices of classical diplomacy all but disappeared, not only in Europe but in the United States, in the First World War era. Agreement had previously existed that the tasks of the soldier and statesman complemented each other as parts of one seamless political process. Karl von Clausewitz, the Germany military theorist, had described war not as an independent phenomenon with a life of its own related to other political events, but as continuation of policy by other means. Widely perceived as not only having failed to prevent the First World War but also having contributed to its coming, the authority and prestige of professional diplomats was undermined. Civilian authorities also further demonstrated that they had lost control of warfare as the fighting settled into a trench warfare stalemate that was as bloody as it was prolonged. The connection of statecraft to war was first obscured and then forgotten as both military and then political leaders concentrated on winning the military struggle. The First World War set a pattern for twentieth-century wars: warfare became much easier to start than to end as wars came to have a separate existence, seemingly unconnected to political goals. Part of the problem was the concept of total war which involved a desire for total victory and the connecting belief that opponents were such barbarians that they must not only be defeated but crushed; such attitudes, almost akin to those of the religious wars of the Middle Ages, left little or no room for either classical statesmen or negotiations.

The Treaty of Versailles was not a "peace without victory" because

Germany and her allies were not part of the negotiations. They, along with the revolutionary Russia, were cast outside the peace settlement; they were not welcomed or included in the community of nations. And thus the seeds of the Second World War were sown, for the peace was dictated by the victors, not negotiated by equals.

Wilson realized that he had made concessions but believed that if only he could get acceptance of the League of Nations that organization would correct those situations at a later time. This is why the tying of the treaty of peace into the League covenant was so important to him. To Wilson the key at Versailles was the League, and the Allies recognized it and took his measure because of it. Because the League of Nations was so important to him, he was easy prey. He could have threatened the Allies with a refusal to guarantee their territorial settlements if they imposed a Carthaginian peace on Germany. But his desire for the League destroyed that option.

President Wilson returned to the United States and submitted the treaty to the United States Senate for its advice and consent. Little apparent opposition existed as to the terms of peace with Germany, but there was criticism of the covenant of the League of Nations, which, because both were in the same document, meant one might cause the defeat of the other.

At this point perhaps a brief review of the League idea might serve a useful purpose. Many people reasoned that if only some sort of machinery for peace had existed in 1914—a place where the Central Powers could have talked to the Allies—that the First World War would not have taken place. During the war, both in Europe and in the United States, groups organized to promote the idea of an organization of nations which would keep the peace. In 1915 the most important American association, the League to Enforce Peace, held its first meeting and elected William H. Taft as its leader. Its objective was the establishment of a League of Nations binding its members to use their economic and military forces against any one of their number that went to war or committed acts of hostility against another of the signatories in violation of international agreements. Many outstanding American leaders of both political parties, including Wilson and Henry Cabot Lodge, gave sympathetic addresses before the group. But while Wilson in principle agreed with the association's leaders, he neither sought their advice nor took them into his confidence. Thus the idea of a League of Nations was not an original Wilson contribution, and the League covenant itself was the product of many minds; Wilson simply became its champion.

Wilson had unnecessarily antagonized the Republican opposition by asking for a Democratic congress in 1918 and by not placing any prominent Republicans on the peace commission to Paris. The "Round Robin" warned that opposition to the League was not minor. But by the time Wilson signed the Treaty of Versailles he was sick of compromises and said "I have found one can never get anything in this life that is worth while without fighting for it." He also said, "The Senate is going to ratify the treaty," and later, "I shall consent to nothing. The Senate must take its medicine." Wilson was in a fighting mood. It has frankly puzzled many historians how an authority on the American constitutional system, an intelligent and astute politician, could have forgotten the Senate's jealous conception of its role in the conduct of foreign policy. Wilson acted as if he were only responsible to public opinion and not to Congress. Congressmen should accept his accomplished feat since the people were with him. "Those senators do not know what the people are thinking."

There remains a strong possibility that increasing physical and mental disabilities contributed to Wilson's incapacity not only to lead but to function at all. Never physically strong, there is speculation that he may have suffered at least two strokes, perhaps three, prior to assuming the presidency; as early as 1915 other problems surfaced, followed by a severe attack of influenza at the Paris Peace Conference in April 1919 and the massive stroke six months later which paralyzed the left side of his body. Edwin Weinstein has argued that Wilson during his presidency, especially in times of stress, displayed common symptoms of cerebral arteriosclerosis, including "diminished emotional control, greater egocentricity, increased suspiciousness and secrecy, and lapses in judgement and memory." Others, however, just as strongly argue that the non-existence of key medical records of Wilson make such speculation impossible to prove. Indeed, present-day Americans, inured to television presentations on presidential health, complete with detailed reports and diagrams, often forget that public reporting and even knowledge of presidential medical problems did not become available until the 1950s. Wilson's difficulties, as well as those of Franklin Roosevelt's in 1945, were concealed from public scrutiny. Thus Weinstein's explanation, while plausible, is not open to final proof. Certainly the president demonstrated signs of physical and mental wear and tear prior to the massive stroke of 1919. If the causes of Wilson's stubbornness and incapacity to lead remain uncertain, the results are much clearer. Wilson, neither in control of events nor as effective a leader in 1919 as in 1915, failed to mobilize public or political support for his policies.

The Senate at that time could be divided into several groups. At one end were the "irreconcilables" led by Senator William Borah. This was a group of 17 (14 Republicans and 3 Democrats) who, while they would if necessary vote for the treaty with reservations simply as a part of their strategy, in the end were against the League under any circumstances. Almost all of this group were quite sincerely convinced that American entrance into the League of Nations would lead the United States into greater difficulties and probably war; and, after all the League was a radical departure from traditional American diplomacy. In the center was the great majority of the Senate (which the Republicans controlled 49–47). This group split further into those who favored strong reservations and those who favored mild reservations. Within this group were both Republicans and Democrats, and the key point to remember is that they did favor the treaty but with reservations. At the other end of the spectrum were the Democrats who unreservedly favored the treaty as it was. The argument then was not between the internationalists and the isolationists; rather it was a contest between those who championed a strong system of collective security and those who favored a more limited commitment in international affairs. As Thomas A. Bailey has pointed out, at all times there were enough senators who favored the treaty in one form or another to secure its passage. The task of Wilson was to find the common ground on which all of these people could stand, and this is where Wilson failed.

The arguments of the limited internationalists, who proved decisive, are as follows: 1) a worldwide system of collective security, they contended, would not work because the other nations would not give up part of their sovereignty by accepting limitations; 2) Article 10, they believed, was a guarantee of the territorial status quo and was bound to cause trouble; 3) they did not believe that the American people were willing to support the sweeping commitments of the covenant; and 4) the covenant would create great dangers to the American constitutional system since questions of peace and war would now rest in the hands of an international agency the United States could not control. In other words, they wanted Congress to decide the degree of American participation in each crisis as the crisis came up; they would make no binding promise to enforce collective security. This procedure was basically the position of Senator Henry Cabot Lodge.

Lodge, of course, has always played the role of the villian in this dispute—perhaps somewhat, but not completely, unjustly. Lodge headed the Republican party in 1920. It appears that he favored the League with reservations; and it just as clearly appears that he did not favor Woodrow Wilson (partly as a result of an argument over the *Lusitania* notes). But to explain Lodge's actions as the result of purely personal dislike of Wilson is to err badly. Lodge was a politician, the leader of a party that felt it was sure to win the presidency in 1920. Only one thing could prevent that victory and that was a split within the Republican party such as had taken place in 1912. Lodge above all did not want that to happen again, but the Republican irreconcilables and William Borah threatened Lodge with just that prospect if the treaty in the form presented by Wilson passed the Senate. Lodge proceeded to rally the Republicans around the arguments of the limited internationalists.

Wilson presented the treaty to the Senate in July 1919. It of course went to the Foreign Relations Committee headed by Lodge and dominated by the Republicans as a result of the election of 1918. Unfortunately for the friends of the League, there was a disproportionate number of irreconcilables (6 of 10 Republicans) on the committee—a number far out of proportion to their actual strength in the Senate (14 out of 49). This meant that the treaty got a very unfriendly public exposure. While the hearings were going on, Wilson decided to appeal to the public. He traveled 2,000 miles in 22 days and delivered 32 major addresses and 8 minor ones. Wilson captivated the public but weakened his health; he collapsed in September 1919; his left side was completely paralyzed as the result of a stroke, and he never recovered his strength.

At a crucial time the League lost its greatest champion. The Senate Foreign Relations Committee reported fourteen reservations along with a resolution suggesting that the Senate adopt the reservations and give its advice and consent to the treaty.

Most of the reservations made explicit the retention of powers by Congress or the government of the United States. Most were comparatively harmless and did not pose great problems (for example, the right to decide for itself what domestic questions the League had no jurisdiction over). One did, however, say Japan was not to receive Shantung. The key reservation was the second, which stated that the United States assumed no obligation to preserve the territorial integrity or political independence of any other country or to employ troops under the treaty without the authority of Congress in each case. Wilson was not completely opposed to compromise since Gilbert Hitchcock did present four reservations approved by Wilson similar to those favored by the mild reservationists. This step is an indication that had Wilson made the effort he might have gotten together with the moderate group; but he did not, and by the time Hitchcock presented his resolutions it was too late because the moderate Republicans had committed themselves to Lodge's program. From his sickbed Wilson said he could not accept the Lodge reservations.

On November 19, 1919, ratification with reservations was voted down 39 to 55 (39 represents 35 Republicans + 4 Democrats; 55 represents 13 Republican irreconcilables + 42 Democrats.) That same day a second vote was taken on the treaty with no reservations and the vote was 38 to 53 (38 represents 1 Republican + 37 Democrats; 53 represents 46 Republicans, including the irreconcilables, + 7 Democrats.) Over four-fifths of the Senate voted for one version or another, but not at the same time.

Obviously, it was a time for compromise. From across the Atlantic came the news that Great Britain would welcome American ratification with or without reservations. Such diverse Americans as Colonel House, Herbert Hoover, William J. Bryan and W.H. Taft urged Wilson to let the Democrats vote for the treaty with reservations. But Wilson stood firm in his belief that reservations would nullify the treaty. He continued to believe the people were with him and that the next election in 1920 should be made "a great and solemn referendum" on the issue. Lodge could not compromise because he was a prisoner of the irreconcilables and the Democrats could not desert Wilson. Wilson wrote in March 1920 ordering his supporters to defeat senatorial approval on Lodge's terms. On March 19, 1920, the last vote was taken on the treaty with slightly revamped Lodge reservations. It was 49 in favor and 35 against (28 Republicans + 21 Democrats; 12 Republicans + 23 Democrats.) Some 21 Democrats did break away from Wilson; had only 7 of the remaining 23 followed suit, the treaty would have passed 56–28. This raises a question: would Wilson have ratified that version by signing it? Remember that the Constitution provides for ratification as a presidential act with two-thirds of the Senate present and concurring. Thus Wilson could have, and in all probability would have, prevented ratification by refusing to sign, and there is no constitutional provision for a congressional over-ride of such an act.

Who was responsible for the defeat? Certainly Lodge and the Republicans share some of the blame since they appeared more interested in the coming political campaign than in the League of Nations. Certainly the irreconcilables, who resorted to every possible trick in order to defeat the League, share the burden. But in retrospect the major share of the responsibility for the Senate's rejecting the treaty with the Lodge reservations must rest on the shoulders of Wilson. Had he been willing to seek a compromise, either early before the Republicans became committed to the Lodge reservations or even later, there is little doubt the Democrats would have supported him and the United States would have entered the League of Nations.

Would American entrance have made a difference? There are three major arguments which support a positive answer to that question: 1) most observers consider the League a desirable goal; 2) many contend that had the United States joined the League that the international organization could have prevented the rise of aggressors in the 1930s; and 3) still others argue that the world of today is a Wilsonian world with the United Nations acting as the center of international life.

But is not all of this too optimistic a viewpoint? Was the League and its promise of collective security the answer? Walter Schiffer has given a good reply: "The League was intended to maintain reasonable and just conditions in the world . . . [but] the idea that a special machinery for the prevention of war was necessary implied a pessimistic assumption that the world's condition still was far from perfect. But without the optimistic assumption that reason and good faith prevailed in the world it could not be hoped that the new regime would work." As far as the prevention of war was concerned, the League's successful functioning depended on conditions that, if they had existed, would have made the organization unnecessary. Was Wilson in his deep faith in mankind looking too far into the future and neglecting the meanness of man and the realities of political life?

And what of collective security itself? Did not the League of Nations concept and does not the United Nations concept have serious weaknesses that led to the failure of one and that seriously weaken the other? Ronald Stromberg in his important book, *Collective Security and American Foreign Policy*, suggests the theory has some wishful thinking in it much like Wilson's. First, nations refused to make the binding commitments necessary to meet those who challenge the system since nations cannot foresee the future. Second, does not the concept depend on a defense of a status quo that not all nations want to uphold? Third, collective security assumes an agreed definition of aggression—but at what point did Hitler commit a clear act, and is it obvious who commits aggression in many disputes? Fourth, by its stress on punishment does it not remove the possibility of compromise? The whole concept has serious problems not easily solved.

Had the United States joined the League, would World War II have happened? This, of course, is an unanswerable question. Anyone who answers is guessing. A good guess is that American entrance would not have prevented the war and might well have brought the war earlier (say in 1931) than it actually came in 1939. Such an earlier entrance might also have cured the depression and changed American history under those circumstances, but this, of course, is purely speculation.

Is today a Wilsonian world in which his ideas predominate? It is more the world of Theodore Roosevelt who envisioned regional security pacts maintaining the balance of power in particular areas. The North Atlantic Treaty Organization is an old-fashioned military alliance, and it was NATO and not the United Nations which became the bulwark against Soviet military expansion after 1948.

The Versailles treaty was only part of the First World War settlement, and it dealt largely with Europe. Other treaties were signed with Hungary, Turkey, and Austria. But East Asia was largely left out except for a clause that gave Germany's prewar concessions in Shantung China to Japan. The protest against that award led to the crucial May Fourth Movement in 1919, which in turn among other things led to the founding of a Chinese Communist party. The Washington Conference of 1921 produced the East Asian segment of the First World War settlement and included much that was not included in the Versailles arrangements. The naval balance of power, the role of Japan, the future of former German possessions in the Pacific, disarmament, and the future of new weapons, for example, were all discussed at Versailles but not settled until later in Washington. That conference developed, as will be seen, out of both international and domestic concerns.

After the adverse vote against the League of Nations in 1920, President Wilson still had one last hope—the presidential election of 1920. The president hoped that the election, "a solemn referendum," would settle the issue by showing that the majority of American people were in favor of the League. He failed to realize that such a referendum was impossible under the American electoral system. The Democratic candidate, James A. Cox, came out for Wilson's program in general and the League of Nations in particular. The Republican candidate, Warren G. Harding, carefully straddled the fence; he could not afford to ignore men of the stature of William H. Taft, Elihu Root, and Charles Evans Hughes, all of whom favored the League and had large followings within the party. Harding's campaign pronouncements, or "bloviations" as he liked to call them, led pro-League supporters to believe that he favored the League. This group indulged in wishful thinking since Harding had twice voted against the League while in the Senate, but the confusion gave them an opportunity to combine high principle with party regularity and thereby vote for Harding. Harding won by the greatest majority in American history. In a poll of 1,500 Republican women taken after the election, 1,200 of them contended that they voted for Harding in the belief that he would take them into a League of

Nations. Actually Harding won his electoral victory because the American people tired of Woodrow Wilson, and a vote against Cox was a vote against Wilson.

Congress ended the war by joint resolution on July, 2, 1921, reserving all rights granted the United States in the Treaty of Versailles and, in August of that year, Harding signed similar arrangements with Austria and Hungary.

No one was quite sure about the policies of the new president. He soon said that the United States would not join the League of Nations. Instead, he promised to work for an Association of Nations. This association would meet from time to time to settle certain specific problems; the problems would be settled without impairing American rights or sovereignty. Harding suggested that perhaps disarmament was one problem for such a conference to settle.

American support of disarmament had a long history going back to an American aversion to standing armies; that dislike seemed to protect American civil liberties from military supremacy. There was also the belief, largely growing out of the First World War, that the existence of a large body of men and arms led directly to war, and that if nations disarmed, the chances for war would diminish. The United States Army had never threatened these principles, but there were those who believed that the growth of the United States Navy made American support of disarmament something of a joke.

Congress had in 1916 passed a naval act calling for the construction of 156 vessels of which 16 were capital ships—battleships and heavy cruisers. These ships were still under construction when the armistice was signed, and by 1921 only one of the capital ships was completed. The British regarded the continuation of the American construction program as a direct challenge: in the words of the young Winston Churchill, "Nothing in the world, nothing that you may think of, or dream of, or any may tell you; no arguments, however strong; no appeals, however seductive, must lead you to abandon that naval supremacy on which the life of our country depends." Britain in 1921 announced plans to build a navy "equal to, or superior to, any other navy." The Japanese in 1920 put into full effect their 8-8 plan whereby they planned two capital ships a year for at least eight years. Where they would get the money no one was really sure. It looked to the world, however, as if a great naval race, on a far more gigantic scale than the Anglo-German competition prior to the First World War, was about to take place.

While the naval race was one source of conflict between the three powers, there was also another source, and this was the Anglo-Japanese Alliance. First signed and directed against Russia in 1902, renewed in 1911, and then directed against Germany, it was to expire, unless renewed, in 1921. The Harding administration believed that since the threats of Russia and Germany had disappeared that the alliance must envision action against the United States. In reality the American government was not worried about having to fight the two powers. What really concerned Americans was that the existence of the alliance probably gave the Japanese support, even though it was unwilling support, of the British in carrying out their aggressive plans in East Asia.

In early 1921 the British held an imperial conference in London and suggested renewal of the Anglo-Japanese Alliance; Canadians, however, registered strong opposition. The British suggested a Pacific conference to the American ambassador, George Harvey (who wore knickers to see the king and made long unfriendly speeches causing some to suggest that he wear longer pants and make shorter speeches). The British hoped they could get the Americans to join the Anglo-Japanese Alliance.

The British proposal merged with the American interest in disarmament. On December 14, 1920, Senator William E. Borah had suggested in the United States Senate that the president work toward an understanding with Japan and Great Britain whereby the three powers would cut their building programs 50 percent. The resolution was at first opposed by Harding, but he later came around and accepted it because he recognized that most Americans were getting tired of spending vast sums of money on this great navy.

While the British proposal was coming across the Atlantic, Secretary of State Charles Evans Hughes had sent a cable to Britain suggesting a disarmament conference in Washington. The two cables probably crossed in the mid-Atlantic; they proposed two different kinds of conferences. Hughes, when he received the British proposal, put the two proposals together and decided to have a conference treating both Pacific problems and disarmament. After beating off a British proposal for a separate Pacific conference, Hughes invited Japan, Great Britain, France, and Italy to come to the disarmament conference, and added Portugal, the Netherlands, China, and Belgium, all of which would attend only the Far Eastern part of the conference.

On November 11, 1921, Harding presided at a colorful ceremony in Arlington Cemetery at the burial of America's unknown soldier. The next day the Washington Conference on the Limitations of Armament began. Harding, in a typical address, welcomed the delegates and pointed out that the hopes of the world centered on Washington. Secretary of State Hughes, it was expected, would make the same type of general welcoming address, but midway through his speech Hughes sternly said that it was time to stop talking about disarmament and do something. He startled the delegates, and indeed the world, by listing 845,740 tons (15 capital ships under construction and 15 other battleships) that the United States was willing to stop construction on or scrap. One can imagine the delight of Japan and Britain, but it was short-lived. Hughes asked the British to stop construction on 583,000 tons (4 ships under construction and 19 existing ones) of capital ships. One British admiral leaned forward in his chair in the "manner of a bulldog, sleeping on a sunny doorstep, who had been poked in the stomach by the unwary foot of a traveling salesman seriously lacking in any sense of the most ordinary proprieties or considerations of personal safety." The Japanese were next. Hughes proposed that Japan scrap 448,000 tons of capital ships (by stopping construction on 6 capital ships and scrapping 17 others). Thus Hughes proposed to destroy a total of 76 ships planned, being built, or built. As one man said, Hughes sank in thirty-five minutes more ships than all the admirals of the world had sunk in a cycle of centuries. Hughes went on to call for a ten-year naval holiday in the construction of capital ships in the ratio of 5-5-3 (roughly 500,000 tons each for the U.S. and Great Britain, with 300,000 for Japan). He later suggested 175,000 tons for France and Italy. Hughes played his trump card at the very beginning of the conference. He captured world opinion, and few nations at the conference were willing to oppose a plan that seemed to have worldwide support.

Where had the plan come from? President Harding had appointed Elihu Root, former secretary of state and elder statesman of the Republican party; Oscar W. Underwood, the Democratic Senate minority leader; and Henry Cabot Lodge, chairman of the Senate Foreign Relations Committee, as delegates along with Hughes. Harding had apparently learned a great deal from Wilson's experience. The delegation, along with Theodore Roosevelt, Jr., the assistant secretary of the navy, very carefully developed proposals for the conference. The navy, of course, did not want to stop the construction program or scrap any of the fleet, and as a result the first proposal was that the United States and Britain have a navy of one million tons apiece. But the American delegation finally scaled the proposal down to half that size. Only eleven men knew of the proposal that Hughes was to make at the conference. Lodge expected Japan to accept the plan but not Great Britain.

At the second session of the conference the other countries accepted the Hughes proposal in "principle." Shortly thereafter Japan began to ask for a ratio of 70 rather than 60 percent, and the argument began. It was hampered by the fact that the Japanese had to telegraph almost everything home to Tokyo and made very few decisions without doing so; this procedure often took several days. Hughes refused to back down and even went so far as to indirectly threaten Japan with an economic boycott. The Japanese suddenly gave their approval but with one important qualification. They would agree only if the Americans would assent, along with the Japanese, not to further fortify their Pacific Islands; this stipulation would apply to the Phillipines, Guam, and Wake on the American side and Formosa, the Pescadores, Amoni-Oshima, and the Bonin Islands and others on the Japanese side. Hughes successfully excluded Hawaii from the scope of the agreement, and this clause became Article XIX of the Five-Power Naval Treaty. Having gained Japan's support, Hughes thought the naval treaty would go through easily, but he had not counted on the French.

France was in an unusual position at the conference. During the race at the turn of the century between Great Britain and Germany, France had chosen to build up an army rather than to join the battleship race; this had remained their policy during and after the First World War. In 1921, France had a very small navy, but did have the world's largest army. At the conference France refused to limit its army unless the American and British governments would guarantee its security against

Germany. This they were unwilling to do, so nothing was done at the Washington Conference about the limitation of land armaments. The French, left out of the discussions on naval armament between the representatives of Great Britain, Japan, and the United State, felt that their prestige was slipping and asked for 300,000 tons of capital ships rather than the 175,000 suggested by Hughes. The conference was almost broken up by this French monkey-wrench. Hughes pointed out that if the French, who then had 164,000 tons, reduced in the same ratio as the others, only 134,000 tons would be given them; rather, the plan suggested 175,000. The ratio in 1921 was 6 to 1 against France, while the plan suggested 3 to 1. Thus France would receive more under the agreement than out of it. This simple arithmetic did not penetrate the French delegation. Hughes finally appealed to the French prime minister, Briand. Briand accepted the 175,000-ton limit but would not accept any limitation on auxiliary ships, light cruisers, destroyers, or submarines. Hughes had hoped to apply the same ratio to all ships, but in order to gain French support of the capital ship agreement, he had to give in on the auxiliary ships and submarines; the Washington Conference did not include quantity limitations on those categories.

To summarize, the Five-Power Naval Treaty (United States, Japan, Great Britain, France, and Italy) imposed a ten-year naval holiday on the construction of capital ships, provided for the scrapping of seventy-one vessels planned, being built, or already built, and set up a ratio of 5-5-3-1.75-1.75 among the five existing fleets. It also provided the Japanese and the Americans would not further fortify their Pacific Islands.

The second key treaty of the conference was the Four-Power Treaty. One of the main goals of the American delegation was to end the Anglo-Japanese Alliance; Britain would have liked the United States simply to come in as the third member of that defensive alliance, but the American delegates, who shuddered every time the word "alliance' arose at the conference, refused. After some broad proposals by the two allies, Hughes, Lodge, and Root came up with a version of the Anglo-Japanese Alliance that stripped it of almost all obligations. This Four-Power Treaty, which also included France simply as a method of raising French morale, pledged the powers to respect each other's possessions in the

Pacific and to confer jointly if disputes among them or aggression from outside threatened the peace. The only obligation was to confer, but there were no enforcement provisions.

The third key treaty of the conference was the Nine-Power Treaty. Signed by all nine powers at the conference (United States, Great Britain, Japan, Italy, France, Portugal, China, the Netherlands, and Belgium), this pledged the powers to respect the sovereignty, independence, and integrity of China, to give China an opportunity to establish a stable government, and to uphold the Open Door in China. For the first time the American policy of the Open Door was accepted by international powers in treaty, that is, in binding form.

The fourth group of agreements pertained to Japan. The Japanese agreed to restore Shantung to the Chinese and to sell the Japanese-owned Shantung railway to the Chinese. Hughes had accomplished what Wilson had failed to do. The Japanese also agreed to withdraw their troops from Siberia, and this they shortly did. Again, Hughes by diplomatic pressure achieved what Wilson had failed to accomplish.

The treaties then went to the United States Senate for its advice and consent. All depended on the Four-Power Treaty which was the only treaty that had aroused a great deal of discussion. This was partly due to the fact that secret negotiations had taken place and that the treaty surprised everyone. The Hearst newspapers led the opposition and they were joined by the Irish-Americans, who were not only distrustful of the Four-Power Treaty but of the naval treaty as well because they were against England. Shortly before the conference, one admiral had said of the Irish-Americans that "they are like zebras, either black horses with white stripes, or white horses with black stripes. But we know they are not horses—they are asses, but each of these asses has a vote, and there are lots of them. . . ." This small but vocal opposition did not worry Henry Cabot Lodge, and here the wisdom of appointing Lodge to the delegation was never more apparent. Lodge's main opposition came from William E. Borah and others of the group classed as irrec-oncilables in the League debate. Thousands of petitions in favor of the treaty poured in—the churches alone sent about eleven million names. Borah and the others still thought it was an alliance, and Borah, an elected representative of the people, retorted that if every man, woman, and child in the United States favored the Four-Power Treaty, he would still vote against it. Borah and his group did put enough pressure on Republicans to force an amendment saying that the treaty envisioned "no commitment to armed force, no alliance, no obligation to join in force." Lodge was wise enough to accept it, and thus Underwood reported to Harding that the treaty would have the support of the Democrats. The treaty passed by a vote of 67 to 27, and the rest of the treaties went through with only token opposition (one vote against).

Since the Second World War it has become fashionable to criticize the Washington agreements. The critics say that the United States gave up naval supremacy badly needed in 1941, that it gave up fortifying key Pacific Islands, and that the United States should have gotten more iron-clad promises against aggression. To indulge in this criticism ignores some basic historical facts. The United States did not yield actual naval supremacy in 1921; it did yield a possible future naval supremacy, but this supremacy could have been gained only if Congress had continued to vote the funds necessary to complete the naval construction program, and there is no indication that it would have done so; indeed, congressmen had not voted such funds for the three years prior to the conference, and they did not even vote the funds in the interwar period to keep the navy up to the treaty level. But, more important, this criticism ignores the fact that if the United States had kept building, Japan and Great Britain would not have stood still; certainly the U.S. would have had a bigger navy in 1928, but Japan would have had a 10-9 ratio with the U.S., not 10-6. Hughes thus obtained equality with Great Britain and supremacy over Japan for ten years—a considerable achievement. Nor was there much chance that Congress would ever have voted the funds to fortify the islands. They had not, and they did not even on the eve of the Second World War. Finally, no iron-clad agreement to stop aggression would ever have passed the Senate, nor was one possible between enemies rather than friends.

Hughes achieved four successes at the Washington Conference. He stopped the naval race, ended the Anglo-Japanese Alliance, negotiated a retreat of Japanese expansion on the Asian continent without fighting a war, and advanced the principle of the Open Door, which was now accepted by all powers. Hughes cleared the air of suspicion between the U.S. and Japan and erected a peace structure in the Far East. That the agreement did not succeed in the long run was not the fault of the Washington Conference but of future American blunders. The conference had settled problems on a realistic basis with each power giving up something and each power gaining something. Perhaps it is relevant to the present and the future that limitations of armaments cannot come without political agreements as well.

Finally, one must ask in conclusion, whether in the American entrance into the "Great War" or at either the Paris Conference or the Washington Conference, American statesmen recognized the historical significance of the First World War. The Great War ended the Columbian Age of history, an age of European domination of the world that had begun with the voyages of Columbus in 1492. An old Greek adage "that those the gods wish to destroy, they first make mad" aptly fits as a description of the peoples who fought that war. Europeans destroyed themselves, and power began to pass to nations outside Europe—the United States, Japan, the Soviet Union. This shift, one that historians will note for centuries to come as one of the hallmarks of the twentieth century— along with nuclear energy and a gigantic increase in world population— was one that Americans did not recognize. It was not until the end of another world war (the Second) that Americans clearly saw the significance of the shift and what it meant to their future. The United States in 1922 was in both an economic and political sense the most powerful nation in the world; militarily it certainly ranked in the first three. But in the 1920s and 1930s, it chose not to recognize the importance of the historical shift in the balance of power but rather to retreat behind oceanic walls. It went from President Wilson determined to control events to leaders just as determined to ignore events. That reaction to Wilsonianism was but one of the man's legacies—others were to come.

Selected Reading

Robert H. Ferrell's *Woodrow Wilson and World War I, 1917–1921* (1985) brilliantly presents the war years. An excellent introduction can also be found in John Milton Cooper, Jr., *The Warrior and the Priest: Woodrow Wilson and Theodore Roosevelt* (1983). David Kennedy re-creates the home front in his *Over Here: The Home Front in the First World War* (1980). *Walter Lippmann and the American Century* (1980) by Ronald Steel presents a good discussion of intellectual currents. Preparedness is covered in *The Citizen Soldiers: The Plattsburgh Training Camp Movement, 1913–1920* (1972) by John Garry Clifford.

Why the First World War military strategies ended in stalemate is best explained in Steven E. Miller, ed., *Military Strategy and the Origins of the First World War* (1985). Frank Freidel's *Over There: The Story of America's First Great Overseas Crusade* (1964) is an interesting introduction. *Captains and Cabinets: Anglo-American Naval Relations, 1917–1918* (1973) by David Trask aptly describes an important naval element. Allan Millett's previously noted book, *For the Common Defense*, is excellent, and a classic book by Charles Seymour, *American Diplomacy During the World War* (1934) remains useful. *No Man's Land: 1918, The Last Year of the Great War* (1980) by John Toland vividly re-creates that crucial year. C.R.M.F. Cruttwell's *A History of the Great War, 1914–1918* (1936) is the best description of the campaigns for the general student reader.

Arthur Walworth treats the armistice negotiations in his *America's Moment: 1918, American Diplomacy at the End of World War I* (1977). Arno J. Mayer presents a broad interpretation in the *Politics and Diplomacy of Peacemaking* (1967). The volume by Harold Nicolson, *Peacemaking, 1919* (1931) is most readable. The critical *Economic Consequences of the Peace* (1920) by John Maynard Keynes should be read in conjunction with Etienne Mantoux's *The Carthaginian Peace or The Economic Consequences of Mr. Keynes* (1952.) Still useful is Thomas A. Bailey's *Woodrow Wilson and the Lost Peace* (1944). Great wisdom can also be found in Hajo Holborn's *The Political Collapse of Europe* (1951).

Thomas A. Bailey's *Woodrow Wilson and the Great Betrayal* (1945) remains the most convincing interpretation of the defeat of the treaty in the United States. Both William C. Widenor's *Henry Cabot Lodge and the Search for American Foreign Policy* (1980) and Robert James Maddox's *William E. Borah and American Foreign Policy* (1969) add other perspectives, as does Carl Parrini's *Heir to Empire: United States Economic Diplomacy, 1916–1923* (1969). Collective Security and American Foreign Policy: From the League of Nations to NATO* (1963) by Roland Stromberg and Walter Schiffer's *The Legal Community of Mankind* (1954) raise important questions about the League of Nations concept.

Roger Dingman's *Power in the Pacific: The Origins of Naval Arms Limitation, 1914–1922* (1976) and Thomas H. Buckley's *The United States and the Washington Conference, 1921–1922* (1970) are solid, competent studies. *After Imperialism: The Search for a New Order in the Far East, 1921–1931* (1965) by Akira Iriye is stimulating.

4 From Bolsheviks to Republicans

While the peacemaking and its attendant struggles had proceeded at both Versailles and Washington, the world scene continued to change dramatically. In particular, a new actor, the Soviet Union, appeared. Not invited to either conference, the new Russian government in 1921 was isolated and feared. Few doubted the Soviet Union would play a role, but whether a revolutionary Marxist one, threatening to many countries, or a more traditional Russian one, largely threatening to close-by neighbors, remained unclear. Possessor of the greatest land mass on the face of the earth, Russia had often seemed more dangerous than its actual performance in world affairs had indicated. But what would happen if that promise turned into performance?

While the Anglo-German naval competition was rising to its peak in the years before the First World War, a British geographer, Halford Mackinder, put forward another theory of power with Russia at its center. In 1904 Mackinder presented a paper to the Royal Geographical Society entitled "The Geographical Pivot of History"; he followed this with a book, *Democratic Ideals and Reality*, aimed at the peacemakers at Versailles in 1919. Mackinder, unlike Mahan, met indifference and his ideas did not become popular until the Second World War; nevertheless, they are of great importance at this point.

Mackinder argued that world power based only on control of the sea would not continue to hold center stage. While he recognized that water covered nine-twelfths of the earth, he contended that a land-based power, which would then use its resources to also build a world navy, would come to dominate the world. Of the three-twelfths of the world composed of land, the World Island (consisting of Europe, Asia, and Africa) made up two-thirds of that whole; on this World Island lived seven-eighths of the world's population. Thus he had an image of a World Island sitting in a world ocean. To Mackinder, the key to the World Island existed in an area which he called the Heartland, which extended from the Volga Basin in western Russia to eastern Siberia, and from the Himalayas in the south to the northern Arctic Sea. Rivers in this area flowed into the frozen arctic or into inland seas; this meant that the pivot area would remain invulnerable to sea power from the surrounding world ocean. From a political viewpoint Russia possessed, with the exception of some East Asian territory, almost all of the Heartland. An arc of coastlands, which Mackinder called the Inner or Marginal Crescent, partly (with the exception of the northern boundary) girded the Heartland. In this area, in which all rivers drained into navigable seas, he included all of continental Europe and the monsoon areas of Asia (India, Southeast Asia, and China). Great Britain and Japan he designated the Outer Islands. The fourth area he labeled the Outer Crescent, and this included the rest of the world. That area incorporated the United States; in 1904 and 1919 Mackinder regarded America of little significance.

Mackinder feared the potential strength of the Heartland. In 1904 he stated: "The oversetting of the balance of power in favor of the pivot state, resulting in its expansion over the marginal lands of Europe-Asia would permit the use of continental resources for fleet building, and the empire of the world would then be in sight." Mackinder at first thought that Germany might eventually control and then use the resources of the Heartland. He formulated a three-point thesis; "Who rules East Europe commands the Heartland; who rules the Heartland commands the World Island; who rules the World Island commands the World."

In Mahan and Mackinder there were two different theories of power; the First World War seemed to vindicate Mahan, and the Second World War seemed to support Mackinder's theories. With Mackinder, however, it is wise to advance slightly into the future and look at his theories at a later date. In 1943, four years before his death, Mackinder wrote that his ideas had more validity than ever. He still believed in the strength of the Heartland, but he then included the United States as a defense in depth for the lands of the Inner Crescent. He concluded with this warning: "All things considered, the conclusion is unavoidable that if the Soviet Union emerges from this great war as conqueror of Germany, she must rank as the greatest land power on the globe. Moreover, she will be the power in the strategically strongest defensive position. The Heartland is the greatest natural fortress on earth. For the first time in history it is manned by a garrison sufficient both in number and quality."

The leading opponent of Mackinder, the American Nicholas J. Spykman, questioned the strength of the Heartland in his book, *Geography of the Peace*. In his study he cited harsh climatic conditions which restricted agricultural production in the Soviet Union; critical coal, oil, and iron resources in indefensible positions on the borders of the Heartland; and geographical obstacles to Russian expansion in the north, south, east, and southwest. Spykman believed the Rimland or Inner Margin (Mackinder's Inner Crescent) of Eurasia more important than the Heartland. He advised that he "who controls the rimland Eurasia then rules Eurasia, and controls the destinies of the world."

By 1919 two different theories of world power competed for attention. As mentioned, the First World War confirmed Mahan, but what would the future bring? If one followed Mahan's theories, one would have to bet on the continued superiority of Great Britain, with perhaps a side bet on the United States; if one followed Mackinder's ideas, one would have to bet on Germany, if she could conquer the Soviet Union. Either way, the future of Russia remained the key element. But Russia, torn by revolution in 1919, represented even more than usual, in the later words of Winston Churchill, "a riddle wrapped in a mystery inside an enigma."

President Wilson had declared in point six of his Fourteen Points that world opinion would regard the treatment accorded Russia by her sister nations as the "acid test" of their good will. Within a few weeks the Soviet government deserted the Allies and made a separate peace at Brest-Litovsk with the Germans on March 3, 1918. The Wilson administration refused to recognize the revolutionary government and withdrew its diplomatic mission to Vologda, where American Ambassador David Francis maintained an unofficial contact with the Soviet authorities. He did this through Raymond Robins, the head of an American Red Cross mission in Moscow, and Madden Summers, the American consul in Moscow. In time the Soviets came to regard Robins and Summers as the official representatives of the United States government. Perhaps the greatest difficulty experienced by the Wilson administration in Russia was the simple fact that it often did not know what was taking place. In addition, it also received conflicting advice: Robins called for cooperation with the Russians, while Summers called for intervention, and Ambassador Francis, while anti-Bolshevik, seemed to favor a policy of inaction. The dangers of such a situation, largely caused by a lack of reliable information, were manifest.

In early March 1918, British and French forces landed at Murmansk in northern Russia in order to protect that key point against attacks from German groups stationed in Finland. The troops landed at the invitation of local Soviet authorities fearful of a German attack; such an attack did not take place. But in response to the perceived threat, an American warship also put 150 American marines ashore to help protect the railroad from Murmansk to Petrograd. The Soviet commissar for war, Leon Trotsky, supported this initial landing when he sent instructions to the local Soviet, "You must accept any and all assistance from the Allied Missions and use every means to obstruct the advance of the plunderers." Trotsky, more than willing to use Allied troops to advance his own purposes, became alarmed when the German threat evaporated and the Allies extended their operations from Murmansk to Archangel. To the Soviets it looked like a Western supported counterrevolution against the Bolshevik regime. Three American battalions of about 4,500 men had joined the Allied forces in September of 1918. With their goal becoming more and more unclear, they had joined the Allies in advancing along the railroad toward Vologda, where the British hoped to meet a division of liberated Czechoslovak prisoners. President Wilson wisely withdrew the American forces from the northern area in June 1919. Wilson did not want the Americans to intervene in Russian internal affairs. Within six months the Soviets succeeded in driving out both the British and the French who undoubtedly did have ideas about influencing the civil war then taking place between the Bolshevists and anti-Bolshevists in Russia. The Russians never forgave the British and French for their support of anti-Bolshevik groups.

A more important intervention, the one which did poison Russian-American relations, took place in Siberia. The forerunner of Allied intervention in this area began with a railway mission sent to Russia in June 1917. One of the most serious problems facing the provisional Kerensky government centered on the threatened collapse of the Russian railway system; of particular concern was the Trans-Siberian system which extended 4,700 miles from Vladivostok to the interior of Russia. As a result of the collapse of the Russian government, thousands of tons of Allied war materials needed by Russian armies fighting the Germans in the west had piled up in Vladivostok. An Allied commission, headed by the American John F. Stevens, set about reorganizing the Russian railroads, including not only the Trans-Siberian but the Chinese Eastern. The commission planned to run the roads for the benefit of Russia and then turn them back to the Russians when political conditions became more settled.

But the chaos that came about as a result of the Bolshevik Revolution of November 1917 made it clear that conditions might not settle down for quite some time. Admiral Kolchak appeared as the leader of the anti-Bolsheviks in Siberia, and the area soon became a hotbed of conflict. By the spring of 1918 no one could say, with any degree of certainty, who controlled Siberia. In the meantime the French and Japanese called for an intervention to take place, and, after the Treaty of Brest-Litovsk, the pressures for an intervention became stronger. Because of the Russian-German treaty the Germans could now withdraw their troops from the Eastern Front to the Western Front, and once that occurred the Allies faced the possibility of a gigantic German offensive. They argued that a Siberian intervention would force the Germans to leave some of their troops on the Eastern Front.

The country most favorably inclined toward intervention in Siberia was Japan. To the Japanese, the Siberian chaos appeared a golden opportunity to expand into a potentially rich area. Wilson loomed as the major opposition to Japanese plans. Wilson refused to support an intervention for two reasons: first, he believed that such a policy would strengthen the extreme revolutionary elements in Russia and would alienate Russian opinion from faith in the United States; second, he believed it contrary to America's democratic war aim of self-determination. Time and again Wilson refused to intervene, and the Japanese hesitated to intervene without American support. But on April 4, 1918, some 500 Japanese marines landed in Vladivostok to "protect" Japanese nationals after the murder of three Japanese merchants.

With the Japanese landing, pressure for American intervention began to increase. Wilson received mistaken reports that released German and Austrian prisoners in the area had armed themselves and attacked Allied troops; again, as in northern Russia, Wilson suffered from incorrect information. In such a confusing situation correct information (like the reports from Captains William B. Webster and W.L. Hicks that the Siberian prisoners did not threaten Allied interests) had a difficult time filtering to the top.

But even the Soviets realized that the American position might weaken and crumble and the Japanese might dramatically increase their stake. Lenin, in order to gain more breathing space, gave a letter to Robins just before the latter left Moscow, suggesting that if America would prevent the Japanese intervention, then the Soviet government would give American capitalists preferred economic rights in Siberia. Lenin hoped this outright bribe would work, and he was not too worried that he would have to make it good. The Wilson administration ignored the letter.

Then on the scene appeared that strange group of soldiers—the Czechoslovak Legion. These troops, Russian prisoners in the Ukraine but released after the Treaty of Brest-Litovsk, had heard that a Czechoslovak nation was arising out of the ruins of Austria-Hungary and wanted to fight the Germans and Austrians to hasten that process. The Allies wanted them to go to Vladivostok and board troop ships for Europe, where they would fight against the Central Powers. The Bolsheviks agreed to let the troops, 40,000 or so, ride the Trans-Siberian Railroad to Vladivostok if the Czechs would give up some of their arms. The Czechs agreed and the long trip began. As luck would have it, the Czechs at one point ran into a group of Hungarians, their former overlords. The Hungarians killed a Czech, and the Czechs hung a Hungarian; the Soviets then arrested the guilty Czechs, but other Czechs then raided the local jail and liberated their comrades. The local Soviets peacefully settled the dispute at that point, but the news of the Czech

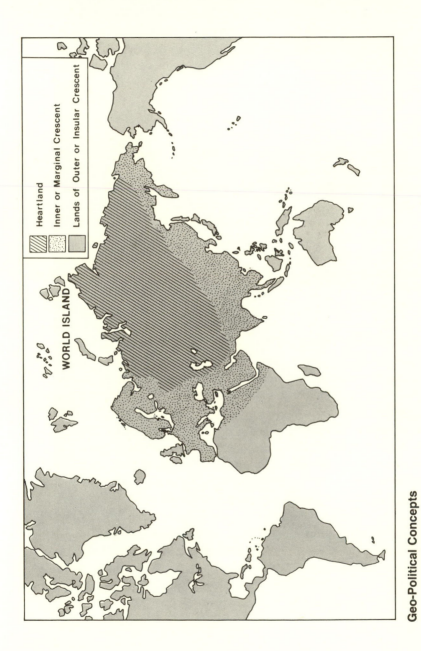

Geo-Political Concepts

action hit hard in Moscow, and orders came down to completely disarm and disband the Czechs. The Czechs decided to fight their way through to Vladivostok, and within a few weeks this well-organized group controlled hundreds of miles of the Trans-Siberian. Soon the Czechs also dominated much of western Siberia, and had become participants in the Russian civil war.

Wilson decided to use the Czechs to fight off the German prisoners apparently arming in the area, and decided that the Czechs would need support from the Allies to do this and also to complete their trip. On July 6, 1918, the president agreed to intervention, the stated reason— to save the Czechs and to protect Allied war supplies at Vladivostok. He informed the Russian people that the Allied intervention did not plan to interfere in Russian internal affairs; the Allies wanted the Russians to regain control of their own affairs. Wilson's public reasons dealt in specifics but left unstated the real reason for American intervention. Wilson hoped that the presence of the American troops would restrain the Japanese and prevent them from actually taking over the entire area. Once assured of the participation of the United States, the Allies moved quickly; by the end of 1918 some 6,400 British, 7,000 American, token French and Italian forces, and 70,000 Japanese troops occupied areas of Siberia. The French and Italians withdrew in 1919, the Americans and British in 1920, and the Japanese, after years of dispute, in 1922.

With little help from Washington, the American commander, General William S. Graves, found himself in a difficult political position. The Czechs clearly did not need protection (and how could 7,000 Americans protect 40,000 armed Czechs since they already controlled a large part of western Siberia by themselves?). No German armed prisoners materialized for the Czechs to fight. Indeed the Czechs had become involved in the Russian civil war and battled against the Bolshevik government. And even if they had sent a full train out every day, it would have taken the Bolsheviks two to three years to move all the supplies at Vladivostok over the Trans-Siberian. This set of circumstances negated the stated reasons for the sending of American troops to Siberia.

The primary task of the American military became the protection of the Trans-Siberian and Chinese Eastern railroads with the intention of returning these to Russian control. In effect, however, improvement of the railroad facilities helped the anti-Bolshevists more than it did the Bolsheviks, since the former controlled most of the territory in Siberia. The Americans found themselves right in the middle—disliked by the Allies for not fully participating in the civil war and disliked by the Russians for showing up at all. As it often does, the United States government tried to take a compromising course and ended up by satisfying no one, as each nation in Siberia had its own political motives. The British and French went there prior to the armistice because they believed their Russian friends would fight against the Germans; after the armistice, unwilling to desert their friends, they concluded that the Bolshevik government represented German interests. The Japanese military group hoped to gain control of eastern Siberia and in particular the vital Chinese Eastern Railroad. American motives self-destructed on a mixture of altruism and lack of knowledge. Wilson tried to restrain the Allies without much success. With the signing of the armistice little reason remained to stay, but Wilson feared that if the American troops left, the Japanese would completely take over. The American public, however, gained the impression that Americans went there to suppress the Bolsheviks. Wilson, hoping for Japanese support of the League, could not bring the clash with Japan into the open. In 1933 when the United States government finally recognized the Soviet Union, the Russians agreed that the United States had indeed intervened to restrain the Japanese and not to overthrow the Soviet government. Needless to say, in later cold war years they changed this opinion.

Good intentions had embroiled Americans in a dispute in which neither the American interest was clear to the American people nor the military action one that could have gained the desired political results. Under unclear circumstances, no overt actions often succeed better than mistaken ones. Activist presidents, such as Wilson, often feel compelled to act when inaction and cautious waiting might well secure better results.

Republican presidents in the 1920s solved the Bolshevik problem by continuing not to have any official relations with Russia at all. Indeed much of the diplomacy of presidents Warren G. Harding, Calvin Coolidge, and Herbert Hoover consisted of either not acting or when they did, with great caution.

After his election in 1920, President Warren G. Harding said that the "League Covenant can have no sanction by us." And no subsequent administration, Republican or Democratic, attempted to take the United States into the League of Nations. Congress in 1921 also said that the United States should "not be represented or participate in any body, agency, or commission" of the League of Nations without the consent of congress. This seemed to cut off any association of the United States government with the League. Nevertheless, of course, the League operated during the 1920s and the 1930s. Secretary of State Charles Evans Hughes, however, made use of "unofficial observers," and through the years the Americans did cooperate with many of the social and humanitarian projects of the League. American representatives made suggestions at some League meetings but never voted and never considered themselves members of the League.

But if no American president asked for American entrance into the League of Nations during the interwar period, every president urged American entrance into the World Court. The World Court, or to use its official name, the Permanent Court of International Justice, came into existence as the creation of a committee (headed, incidentally, by the American Elihu Root) appointed by the League of Nations Council to draw up a plan for a new world court. Readers should distinguish the World Court from the Hague Court of Arbitration; the latter consisted simply of a panel of judges willing to serve as arbitrators for a specific dispute, while the former involves a true permanent court with judges serving elected terms. To this World Court nations might refer general disputes; or agree in advance to submit certain types of disputes, such as the interpretation of a treaty, if such a dispute should arise; or the court could give either an advisory decision or final judgment on any question referred to it by the League. A majority vote of the fifteen judges, no two from any one nation, would determine decisions. Harding submitted the World Court protocol to the Senate in 1923, but he died before a vote was taken.

Harding's successor, Calvin Coolidge, also recommended American participation, but the same tactics used against the League, delay and reservations, defeated American entrance into the World Court. Henry Cabot Lodge and later William E. Borah denounced the Court as a tool of the League of Nations. In 1925 the House of Representatives went on record as favoring the court by a vote of 302-28. Not until 1926 did the Senate approve it, but with five reservations, 76-17. The League accepted the first four reservations: (1) acceptance of the Court Statute would not involve the United States in any legal relationship with the League; (2) Americans would participate equally with members of the League in the election of judges; (3) the United States would pay its fair share of the expenses of the Court as determined by Congress; (4) the Court statute would not be amended without American consent. The League rejected the fifth amendment which said that the Court could not "entertain any request for an advisory opinion touching any dispute or question in which the United States has or claims an interest" without the consent of the United States government. Coolidge thereafter displayed no more interest in the subject.

In 1929, at the age of eighty-four, Elihu Root worked out a formula that appeared to guard American interests in the judgment of advisory opinions. When the League informed the United States government of an opinion involving American interests, the League would then give the administration a chance to negotiate; if the government remained dissatisfied, the United States could then withdraw from the case. Herbert Hoover accepted the Root formula but, overwhelmed by the depression, did not push the issue; nor did President Franklin D. Roosevelt until 1935. It looked as if the Court statute would pass the Senate until the Hearst press and Father Coughlin began to influence wavering senators against ratification. By a vote of 52-36 (a vote of 59 to 29 would have fulfilled the two-thirds requirement) the Court statute failed to pass the Senate. Again, American participation in an international organization failed by seven votes. Again, a small vocal minority had succeeded in the United States Senate.

The limitation of naval armaments, however, continued to have support. During the Coolidge administration it appeared that the United States and Great Britain were beginning to drift into a new naval race. The Washington Conference had succeeded in limiting only capital ships, that is, battleships and battle cruisers. Eager to extend the Washington ratios to other categories of ships, in 1927 the president sent representatives to a conference in Geneva. The meeting failed since the French and Italians refused to attend, and the Americans, British, and

Japanese could not agree on whether 10,000-ton or 7,500-ton cruisers would benefit their naval strategies. After six weeks the conference broke up, and in 1929 Congress passed a bill calling for the construction of fifteen 10,000-ton cruisers.

The year 1930 saw the last serious attempt at naval limitation at the London Naval Conference. In this treaty, the United States, Great Britain, and Japan accepted a 10-10-6 ratio in heavy cruisers with 180,000 tons, 146,800 tons, and 108,400 tons respectively; in light cruisers a 10 (143,500), 10 (192,000), 7 (100,450) ratio and tonnage; in destroyers a 10 (150,000), 10 (150,000), 7 (105,500) ratio and tonnage; and in submarines a 10 (52,700), 10 (52,700), 10 (52,700) ratio and tonnage. While the French and Italians would not accept limitations on their fleets in those categories of ships, they did accept a five-year extension of the ten-year naval holiday for capital ships provided for in the Washington Conference agreement. Because British naval strength depended in part on what the French and Italians might do, the London treaty included an "escalator clause," whereby if a nonsignatory party built enough ships to threaten Britain's security (or that of Japan or the United States), all powers might exceed the London quotas. This treaty passed the Senate by a vote of 58-9.

As a result of a relaxation of tension after the Washington Conferencer, a blossoming friendship temporarily developed between the Japanese and Americans. The Japanese, impressed by the immediate American aid sent to Japan in 1923 when Tokyo suffered a great earthquake, reciprocated with more cherry trees for Washington, D.C. to join those first sent in 1912. But in 1924 Congress trampled all this good work by excluding all immigration by orientals to the United States.

Previous Japanese immigration to the United States had been regulated by the Gentlemen's Agreement of 1907 made by Theodore Roosevelt. In this agreement the Japanese themselves agreed to exclude Japanese laborers from the United States, a sort of face-saving device. This had drastically curbed Japanese immigration, but loopholes remained. Picture brides, for example, received much publicity from worried progressive reformers. Japanese men in the United States secured wives by picking them from photographs, arranging a proxy marriage in Japan, and then bringing the bride, sight unseen, to the United States, which did not exclude relatives of Japanese already in the United States. The Japanese government prohibited this practice in 1920, but some Americans demanded even more restrictions. Such diverse groups as Californians, worked up about Japanese landowning in the state; the American Federation of Labor, worried about Japanese competition; and the new American Legion, looking for things to worry about, began to put pressure on Congress. Soon the demand for Japanese exclusion began to merge with a larger demand to limit all immigration to the United States from all countries.

In 1917 Congress had passed, over President Wilson's veto, an act which required all immigrants to take a literacy test; everyone over sixteen years of age had to read English or some other acceptable language. But further, an immigration act of 1921 limited immigration from each nation to 3 percent of that nationality living in the United States in 1910; this was tightened up in 1924 to 2 percent of the 1890 census. The 1924 act not only discriminated against eastern and southern Europeans but also excluded anyone ineligible for American citizenship. According to Supreme Court decisions of 1922 and 1923, Japanese, Chinese, and other orientals did not meet American eligibility requirements.

Secretary of State Hughes pointed out the terrible mistake Congress had made in the exclusion provision. If Japan had a quota, like other nationalities, such a restriction would admit about 250 Japanese a year to the United States, a number which was certainly no threat to 130 million Americans. Hughes invited the comments of the Japanese ambassador in Washington, Hanihara Masanao. Hanihara, after consulting with the head of the Far Eastern Division of the Department of State, John Van MacMurray, in an otherwise discreet letter, wrote one unfortunate phrase. He said that "grave consequences" might result from the exclusion. Senators such as Henry Cabot Lodge, ironically one of the architects of the Washington agreements, regarded this as a threat and crushed an administration bill to cut out the exclusion provision by a vote of 76-2. In a letter to a friend, Hughes wrote, "It is a sorry business and I am greatly depressed. It has undone the work of the Washington Conference and implanted the seeds of an antagonism which are sure to bear fruit in the future. . . . The question is not one of war but of the substitution of antagonism for cooperation in the Far East, with all that involves. Our friends in the Senate have in a few minutes spoiled the work of years and done a lasting injury to our country." Hughes thus recognized the Japanese exclusion clause as a major blunder on the part of the United States Senate.

Having insulted the Japanese, the Americans also proceeded to create antagonism across the Atlantic with their position on the war debt question. During the First World War, the Wilson administration had loaned about $7 billion to the Allies; after the war it loaned about $3.3 billion more for relief and reconstruction. Some twenty countries owed the United States government about $10.3 billion. There is little doubt that during this period both the United States and the Allies considered this sum of money as a simple loan at 5 percent interest. To many Americans, the Allies gained territory and reparations at Versailles, while the United States government did not demand the same rewards but did ask for the repayment of the loans. As Calvin Coolidge is reputed to have later dryly remarked, "They hired the money, didn't they?"

But if the average American expected the loans to be repaid, Europeans hedged. They contended that they carried the heavy load in the war (the British, for example, had loaned more money to their allies than they, the British, had borrowed from the Americans) and that whereas the United States had spent money, the Allies had spent the blood of their men. Thus both sides had made a contribution to a mutual effort. Europeans would cancel all of the war debts between all of the Allies. They also pointed out that most of the money had profited both American business and the American government who collected taxes. But while the United States government would not consider cancellation, the American treasury would lower the interest rate to 3.3 percent and let the Allies take sixty-two years to pay.

Given this American attitude, the Allies, to the great discomfort of the Americans, began to connect war debts with German reparations. No American administration would recognize the connection between the two, but the Allies decided that they would not pay the United States until the Germans paid them. As a result of the Versailles treaty the Germans found themselves with a reparations bill of $33 billion plus interest. But the simple fact remained that the Germans found it hard to meet their payments and stabilize their economy at the same time. Germany soon fell into default, and in 1923 the French occupied the Ruhr in an attempt to get something of value from the Germans. In 1924 a committee headed by an American, Charles G. Dawes, devised a plan under which reparations from Germany would continue with smaller scaled-down payments at first, but then would increase year by year as the German economy got back on its feet. This worked until 1930 when the Young Plan, created by an American, Owen D. Young, went into effect. In this plan Germany over a 59-year period would pay some $9 billion in principal and $17 billion in interest; this meant a reduction from the original $33 billion principal. But this plan made the relationship between war debts and reparations explicit. Germany's supposed ability to pay the bill out of its economy remained at the core of the schedules, but the Germans found it easier to pay by borrowing from abroad.

In the period from 1924 to 1931 the Germans paid $2.75 billion in reparations. In that same period, the national and local German governments, plus German industry, borrowed about $4.5 billion of which half came from the United States. In that same period, the United States government received about $2 billion in payment from the Allies on war debts. As the money went round and round in this financial fairyland, everyone felt satisfied. The danger in all of this, that sooner or later American funds might stop going to Germany, materialized with the American stock market crash of 1929. That collapse helped lead to a depression in Germany that in turn helped to bring on Hitler. One remarkable aspect of this is that the only way the rest of the world could pay off its debts to the United States, or that Germans could pay off the principal on the reparations, was to sell goods to the American market. But all during this era the American government proceeded to raise its tariff rates; even with a major depression, the rates continued upward. And, of course, other countries raised their rates, making it just as hard for Americans to sell goods overseas.

In 1931 President Hoover announced a one-year moratorium on war debts, but Congress expected the payments to resume at the end of 1932. In 1932 the European Lausanne Conference wrote off 90 percent of the German war reparations. After this date only token payments on the First World War debts ever found their way to the United States Treasury; Finland, famed as the only nation to completely pay off her debts, gained very little because the American government stood by while the Soviet Union invaded Finland in 1940. But Americans felt that they had learned a lesson out of the whole experience. They would never again, by the terms of the Johnson Act of 1934, loan money to any government which had defaulted on its loan. Needless to say, the United States government might well have written off the loans in the first place, as the Europeans had suggested, as the American contribution to a common war effort.

The United States had now failed to enter the League of Nations, or the World Court, or settle the war debt problem. Limitation of armaments seemed the only successful pursuit. But one other major attempt to gain peace in the 1920s, the Kellogg-Briand Pact of 1928, (or more correctly, the Pact of Paris) is of some importance.

The pact had a strange background. A Chicago lawyer by the name of Salmon O. Levinson had offered a plan to outlaw war in 1921, which gained him the support of many liberals of the day; more important, he also received the support of anti-League people like William E. Borah. Another group led by Nicholas Murray Butler, the president of Columbia University, and Professor James T. Shotwell, worked for the "renunciation of war as an instrument of national policy." While seeking almost exactly the same goal as the former group, the latter group primarily included pro-League supporters.

In 1926 Butler had an opportunity to discuss his plans with the French prime minister, Aristide Briand. In April 1927 Briand made a speech in which he stressed the ties of friendship between the two nations and suggested an agreement outlawing war between the two countries. Of course Briand had more on his mind than he really said. Looking for ways to improve French security against Germany, he hoped to sign a treaty with the United States government which would at least insure that the United States would remain neutral in the event of any future struggle involving France. In other words, the French were proposing a type of negative alliance, for if the French could not secure the Americans in a positive alliance as their ally, then perhaps they could make sure that the United States remained neutral and did not join the

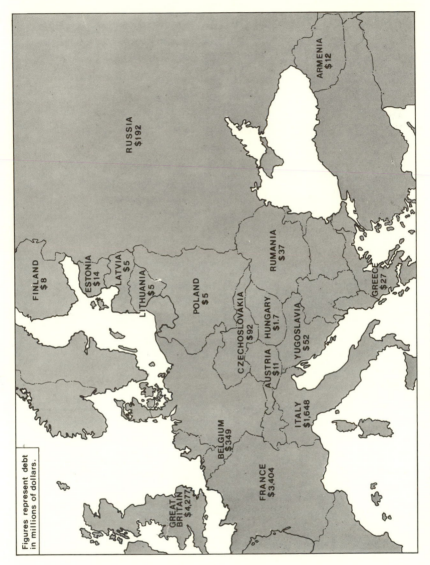

Figures represent debt in millions of dollars.

FINLAND $8

ESTONIA $14

LATVIA $5

LITHUANIA $5

RUSSIA $192

POLAND $5

CZECHOSLOVAKIA $92

AUSTRIA $11

HUNGARY $1.7

RUMANIA $37

YUGOSLAVIA $52

ARMENIA $12

GREECE $27

ITALY $1,648

BELGIUM $349

FRANCE $3,404

GREAT BRITAIN $4,277

European Indebtedness to the United States

side of Germany. Briand's proposal went unnoticed at first until Butler called attention to it in the *New York Times*. Soon a great public clamor for such a pact went up.

Secretary of State Frank B. Kellogg wasn't too sure that he appreciated Briand appealing over the head of the Coolidge administration to the American public, but he decided to remain quiet. Unfortunately for Kellogg, Charles A. Lindbergh chose that particular moment to fly his "Spirit of St. Louis" airplane across the Atlantic (May 1927), and Franco-American friendship suddenly shot to an all-time high. Kellogg realized he would have to move. In June he received an unofficial proposal from Briand for a "Pact of Perpetual Friendship."

Kellogg saw through the plan of Briand and after six months of twisting and squirming came up with an alternate proposal. He suggested to Briand that it would be selfish of them not to share such a noble idea; rather, France should join the United States in asking all the nations of the world to sign a multi-lateral pact renouncing war as an instrument of national policy. Briand became the delayer since he did not want to enter such a pact. While he delayed, other nations indicated their acceptances. Almost all of them accepted with one reservation or another. For example, the United States, as well as Germany, interpreted the pact to mean that they still had the right of self-defense. Signed by fifteen nations in 1928, the pact condemned "recourse to war for the solution of international controversies" and renounced war "as an instrument of national policy," and the signatories agreed to settle all disputes by "pacific means." Eventually over sixty nations, including Germany, Japan, and the Soviet Union, signed the pact. Approved in the United States Senate with a reservation that the United States assumed no obligations to punish violators of the pact, it seemed a major accomplishment to many Americans. Only one senator voted against it.

What was the significance of the pact? The most perceptive writer on the pact, Robert Ferrell, concludes it "was the peculiar result of some very shrewd diplomacy and some very unsophisticated popular enthusiasm for peace." Public opinion, believing peace so easily defined and secured, thought the agreement marvelous. It proved all but useless in the face of aggression in the 1930s, but did have two surprising results. Kellogg, who as indicated had initially not favored the agreement, won a Nobel Peace Prize in 1929. An even greater surprise, at least to the Germans, came in 1946 to Nazi war criminals tried at the Nuremburg Trials and executed for breaking the terms of the Kellogg-Briand Pact.

"Isolationism" is always the key descriptive word applied to the interwar period when discussing the conduct of American foreign relations. It raises, however, an incorrect image of Americans having no relationships with the rest of the world. Clearly, as the descriptions in this chapter indicate, even when centering on political isolation, the traditional use of the word ignores such clear political steps as the naval limitation conferences and the Kellogg-Briand Pact. What falls within, and outside, the scope of the policy of isolationism as practiced in the 1920s and 1930s? First, isolationism did *not* include economic, commercial, or cultural isolation. Americans continued to seek overseas trade and investments, and to have artistic and literary exchanges. Second, isolationism did describe a desire for an unrestricted, independent freedom of political and diplomatic action, a type of unilateralism. Third, isolationism did not involve negative doubts about the limits of American power to influence events, rather it involved a positive decision of a lack of interest in events taking place elsewhere in the world. In other words, a feeling of invulnerability powered isolationism rather than any feeling of vulnerability to outside events. Fourth, isolationism included an enormous disillusionment with the course and outcome of the First World War. The world had not been made safe for democracy and Americans felt betrayed. Perhaps they had learned too much from the experience in the Great War; they might better have studied the words of Mark Twain: "Remember to learn no more from a situation than is in it. A cat that sits on a hot stove will not sit on a hot stove again. But he won't sit on a cold one either." Burned once in international affairs, Americans were reluctant to reach out again; the burdens of the Great Depression reinforced such feelings. Perhaps the Democrats and a new author, Franklin Roosevelt, could change the plot in the 1930s.

Selected Reading
George F. Kennan's two volumes, *Soviet-American Relations, 1917–1920, Russia Leaves the War* (1956) and *The Decision to Intervene* (1958), deal with the American intervention in Russia, as does his *Russia and the West Under*

Lenin and Stalin (1960). Books by Betty M. Unterberger and Richard W. Ullman, *America's Siberian Intervention* (1956) and *Anglo-Soviet Relations, 1917–1931,* 3 vols. (1961–1971), add a fuller picture. N. Gordon Levin, Jr., *Woodrow Wilson and World Politics: America's Response to War and Revolution* (1968) puts the intervention in a broader context.

A definitive work on the diplomacy of the interwar period has not yet been written. A brief survey by L. Ethan Ellis, *Republican Foreign Policy, 1921–1933* (1968) contains an outline, but a student must go to specific monographs for more information. Robert Ferrell's *Peace in Their Time: The Origins of the Kellogg Briand Pact* (1952), *American Diplomacy in the Great Depression* (1957), and *Frank B. Kellogg and Henry L. Stimson* (1963) in the *American Secretaries of State* series carefully cover the late 1920s. Important themes can also be found in Joan Hoff Wilson's *American Business and Foreign Policy, 1920–1933* (1971) and *Herbert Hoover: Forgotten Progressive* (1975). Melvyn Leffler's *The Elusive Quest: America's Pursuit of European Stability and French Security, 1919–1933* (1979) is an excellent piece of work. On East Asia, Dorothy Borg's *American Policy and the Chinese Revolution, 1925–1928* (1947) is an important volume. Richard D. Burns and Edward M. Bennett, eds., *Diplomats in Crisis: United States-Chinese-Japanese Relations 1919–1941* (1974) is filled with sketches of important statesmen. Two biographies remain useful: Merlo J. Pusey's *Charles Evans Hughes,* 2 vols. (1951) and Elting E. Morison's *Turmoil and Tradition: The Life and Times of Henry L. Stimson* (1960). Kenneth J. Grieb has the best recent work on Latin America in his *The Latin American Policy of Warren G. Harding* (1976). William Kamman, *A Search for Stability: United States Diplomacy Toward Nicaragua, 1925–1933* (1968) and Lester D. Langley, *The United States and the Caribbean in the Twentieth Century* (1980) are also solid pieces of scholarship.

5 A National Strategy, 1914–1932

The First World War, the Bolshevik controversy, and the Republican responses of the 1920s displayed the divisions that existed in the United States over the proper use of force in international relations. War has repeatedly played an important part in the course of American history, but Americans have also just as consistently displayed an ambivalence about war and the use of power in the international arena. The use of power to gain political ends, so often bloodily used by Europeans, appeared to Americans unclean, even immoral. From the American Revolution in 1776 through the First World War, Americans had taken part in six major struggles (Revolutionary War, War of 1812, Mexican War, Civil War, Spanish-American War, and First World War), professing every foot of the way their unwarlike nature and rationalizing that they fought defensively to protect themselves from danger. Victories confirmed that Divine Providence supported and made both American goals and war moral. Founded, in part, as a refuge for moralists, it was not long, however, before legalism also became a major component of American culture. While moralism saw war as immoral and unjust (unless of course it was a war for a just cause), legalism offered the view that most conflicts could be adjudicated on the international level through much the same process that lawyers, increasingly American's dominant class, handled arguments on the domestic level. Both views supported the belief that the application of moral principles and rational intelligence to international problems could, should bring about the end of warfare. Peace, it was argued, represented the normal state of mankind, not war; pacifists viewed war as an aberration, one whose time for abolishment had come. An organized, educated public opinion would make this possible. Others, however, less sanguine, pointed out that history recorded wars occurring in almost every year of human history. Until war was indeed abolished, might it not reflect prudence to have a military establishment that could defend the country against those less enlightened about the ultimate futility of war? War appeared to most Americans to be something like poverty: a condition that no one wanted but a fact of life that might well come, a condition that must be faced with courage, and with the proper application of intelligence and foresight a condition that could be conquered and, with a little bit of luck, even avoided altogether. But thinking about war and its attendant problems was not a major concern of most Americans except in wartime.

This ambivalence of the American approach—between those on the one hand who abhorred war and actively worked against it, reflected in the Washington Conference on the Limitation of Armaments and in other diplomatic attempts to secure peace, as well as in the organized pacifist movement, and those on the other hand who believed that in a less than rational world that some degree of military preparedness was necessary—resulted in not only a "born-again" pursuit of peace, but in a continuing reluctance to develop a strong standing military force or even to think about a military strategy. Americans depended, as always, on a volunteer military force and on a military strategy that would be developed as events unfolded. Both factors counted on the existence of enough time to bring the manpower and industrial might of the United States to bear; only then, it was believed, by the population at large, would a military strategy become necessary. In the event of actual war, however, the lack of national military strategy could give an advantage to an enemy who had specific political goals and a military strategy designed to obtain those ends.

Despite this reluctance, nevertheless, as noted in Chapter 1, the United States Navy at the turn of the century had stepped into the strategic vacuum and developed a national security policy based largely on the theories of Alfred Thayer Mahan. The eminent military historian Walter Millis later noted that the new American navy was begun "almost by accident and in absent-mindedness." He, while not an advocate of the naval prowess of the United States, did see the Mahan years as significant. The significance was found not in battleships but in the emergence of a highly trained, technically expert elite that had begun to guide the American military machine. The Dick Act of 1903 created a general staff and a National Guard system and made possible an increase in the size of the army. Elihu Root as secretary of war helped to push the army toward a reorganization that would make for a more professional and managerial officer corps.

With the enhanced management skills of the American military came bureaucracy and an increase in the number of military and civilian support personnel. In 1916 there were 179,376 men in uniform in the services. Two years later the number had grown to 2,897,167. In the same period of time, 450,000 civil servants were hired by the national government, and a great part of them were in war-related positions. At the end of the war 40 percent of them remained on the government payroll. This growth in the size of government left in place the infrastructure for future expansion if a crisis were to demand it. It also created the bureaucratic foundation that would endure and make possible a future national security structure.

An army of the size necessary to wage war in Europe had to be created by conscription. The "Preparedness" theme of Congress in the early months of the First World War was easily adopted by a nation under a cloud of fear. Mahan had also made preparation for foreign battlegrounds a tenet of his doctrine, although he assumed mighty ships would wage battles to preclude mighty armies from having to do so. It was this sense of impending involvement that made mass conscription politically acceptable. Shortly after the declaration of war in April 1917, Congress moved to create the first national army in American history.

The Great War saw many innovations in military machinery. Walter Millis notes three as being decisive: the military airplane, the tank, and automotive transport. The importance of the ground vehicles was not integrated into American planning for several years. It was developments in the automotive industry and with internal combustion engines that allowed the United States to convert that technology to war preparation at a later date. The airplane was a different matter. If the Italian air general, Guilio Douhet, was known in Europe as the "Mahan of the air," it would not be long before his American counterpart would emerge. Technology continued to precede strategy. The boundaries were becoming clearer for the inevitable debate following the war over weapons of the future. As is often the case, the weapons were less the cause of controversy than were the men who wished to use them.

To the military establishment the First World War seemed to validate Mahan's ideas; victory always tends to bring confidence. But the navy actually did little to alter the outcome of the Great War. The years between 1914 and 1918, however, saw American commerce expand dramatically and that, more than any military venture, changed the nature and world stature of the United States in the postwar period. The decision by the Senate to reject an international or multilateral approach to peace-keeping provided a signal to the military that in order to protect its worldwide interest and its newly expanded foreign trade, the United States would depend on a navy second-to-none rather than upon alliances. Of course the possibility existed that public opinion might turn toward isolationism, but the navy failed to deal with that contingency in its planning.

Following the Armistice in 1918, Europe fell into an uneasy peace. The war had stripped Germany of her imperialistic plans, had rendered Russia temporarily impotent under its new Soviet government, and left both Britain and France drained and weak. Japan seemed the only country left with the ability to challenge the United States and then only in the western Pacific. Governed by Mahan's assumptions, the navy could not imagine a country without a powerful navy threatening the United States. With the exception of Great Britain, European navies could not raise a challenge to anyone outside of the Atlantic Ocean. Only the Japanese had the fleet to interdict shipping lanes in the Pacific, and this ability made the Japanese at least a theoretical enemy of the United States. Prior to the First World War, the Japanese and American governments had signed several agreements that had eased tensions. These protected American interests in the Philippines, but they also conceded to the Japanese freedom elsewhere in East Asia. That temporary protection for the Philippines, amounted, in the long run, to no protection at all.

Japanese ambitions in the Pacific grew during the First World War. In 1915, the Japanese government presented the Twenty-One Demands which would have subjugated much of China to Japanese control, but the Chinese successfully resisted. Secretary of State Robert Lansing negotiated an accord with the Japanese foreign Minister, Ishii Kikujiro, which recognized the Open Door policy of the United States in China, while conceding that the Japanese had their own special interests in China. In the peace conferences after the war, as noted, the Japanese had demanded territory from the Chinese and temporarily had occupied Shantung. They also acquired several islands in the Pacific that they had taken from the Germans during the war—the Marshalls, Marianas, and the Carolinas. The United States government retained Yap Island in the Carolinas but acceded to Japan in her other demands. The Japanese landed troops at Vladivostok, in the newly forming Soviet Union, and the American Expeditionary Force in Siberia served notice to the Japanese that the United States would not tolerate any territorial claims in Russian Siberia.

Since the turn of the century, two basic goals had constituted the Pacific Ocean and East Asian policies of the United States—defense of the Philippine Islands and maintenance of the Open Door policy in China. The Japanese possession of an extensive string of potential military bases between the Hawaiian Islands and the Philippines placed American interests at risk. The fact that the British had secretly agreed in 1917 to support Japanese claims to the German islands in the Pacific in exchange for Japanese destroyer support in the Mediterranean did not help Americans feel secure about future British support in the Pacific. Concessions that the Americans and British gave to the Japanese, beginning in 1905, allowed them to expand their influence and bases and by 1919 posed a clear threat to both American goals in Asia.

In early 1919, U.S. Navy Captain Harold E. Yarnell completed a study of potential military conflicts at the request of the General Board and concluded that only Japan posed a viable threat to the United States. Japan had no support bases within its fleet's striking distance to threaten the mainland of the United States, but the United States had several bases across the Pacific from which its fleet could operate and even threaten the ability of the Japanese to trade and, hence, survive. To the American navy, this situation, in the absence of any alliance with Great Britain or any Asian powers, meant that the mission of the navy in East

Asia would follow Mahan's dictum and extend defensive force into the far Pacific with a powerful offensive battle fleet.

In response to the lead by the navy, the army proposed to Wilson's secretary of the navy, Josephus Daniels, that the military departments should draw war plans and create a defense program aimed at the Japanese. Secretary Daniels agreed. Hence, in the immediate postwar period, during demobilization, both services envisioned eventual conflict with the Japanese in the Pacific Ocean. The strategy depended primarily on a fleet in being, consisting of forty-eight battleships and supported by a series of military support bases throughout the Pacific Ocean. Defense of the bases from inland attack and landing assault, where necessary, rested with the army. The Philippine Islands, the farthermost base, represented both the key to this defense and the most difficult place for the army to conduct a major campaign. In 1909, after considerable debate, the army and navy had agreed on the impossibility of defending against a ground attack at Subic Bay; only Manila Bay appeared to offer a reasonable, defensible base for the navy, and even it raised severe logistical problems. Moreover the Joint Board agreed to locate the primary naval base for the Pacific Ocean in the Hawaiian Islands at Pearl Harbor. Hence the Philippines became the outpost of the East Asian security forces of the United States rather than their anchor. The Joint Board and the White House both seemed to find the plans for the Philippines reasonable and feasible.

Even as the nation returned to normalcy and began to seek solace in isolationism, the military prepared to confront a potential adversary 8,000 miles away with a strategy of prewar vintage that did not include, among other things, a role for the airplane. The broad use of aircraft during the First World War initially had little postwar impact on the plans of the Joint Board. The national strategy and vision of power based on a large battle fleet passed unaltered from the first to the third decades of the twentieth century. The transition from two dimensions of military power to three dimensions proved too great for the Joint Board and much of the military leadership to accommodate in so short a time.

In its introduction to combat, the airplane had not failed. In fact its use went far beyond its initial role as a reconnaissance device under the

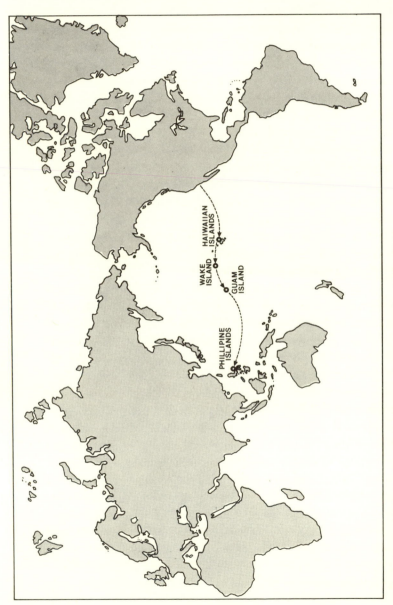

United States Military Resupply Routes in the Pacific, 1914–1941

control of the Army Signal Corps. The airplane became a bomber of considerable ability, it cleared the skies of enemy reconnaissance craft, and it showed promise in direct support of ground forces. In 1914, when the airplane officially became a part of the American military structure, few expected that its role would go beyond that previously assigned to lighter-than-air craft used for decades to provide aerial spotting for artillery or ground troops. Elsewhere, the airplane had received a warmer welcome. Great Britain had created the Royal Air Force shortly after Louis Bleriot flew across the English Channel from Calais to Dover in the summer of 1909. As early as 1911, the American navy talked about the airplane as part of its coastal defense, and U.S. Navy Captain Bradley Fiske, that same year, proposed the airplane as a defensive weapon to protect the fleet in the Philippines.

Captain Fiske used the naval doctrine of Mahan to justify his proposal, but the navy could not see the craft as anything beyond a reconnaissance device. Navy Captain Washington Irving Chambers built a platform on the deck of the cruiser *USS Birmingham,* and in late 1910 a plane flown by Eugene Ely successfully took off from it. A few months later Ely landed on a similar deck on the cruiser *USS Pennsylvania* anchored in San Francisco Bay. Fiske in 1912 patented the first torpedo launched from an airplane; soon thereafter, following two years of trials, a catapult launched an airplane from a naval vessel at sea. Captain Chambers, at the request of the General Board, chaired a study group to examine the role of aircraft in the navy. When the study group issued its report in late 1913, it envisioned naval air as an offensive arm of the navy but used to enhance, not replace, the main battle fleet. All of these attempts to advance the role of the airplane in the navy faced an obstacle created by one major consideration. The battleship fleet cost so much that the navy could not afford extensive research and development of new and, to it, unproven weapons systems. The doctrine of naval commanders, confirmed by successive presidents and congresses, centered on the battleship as the key offensive-defensive weapon of the United States. The army did not dissent.

As Europe went to war in 1914, the United States still could not reconcile the new aeronautical technology to its strategic doctrine. In June 1916 the Navy General board stated that, "aeronautics does not offer a prospect of becoming the principal means of exercising compelling force against the enemy." To underscore the board's point, Secretary Daniels argued against a budget item of $1,187,600 for naval aviation in the 1916 budget request. This came despite effective European use of aircraft for the first two years of the war. Congress authorized $1,000,000, and the navy chose to use the money for coastal defense rather than to enhance fleet operations with aircraft. During the war an attempt to fund the construction of the first American aircraft carrier floundered when the navy internally rejected the idea because it would detract from efforts to create the 48-battleship fleet it still longed for. The navy even disbanded the fledgling Office of Naval Aviation in mid-1919 as the nation returned to peacetime status.

The inevitable demobilization following the war cost the air components of the navy and the army dearly. Despite an air engagement over St. Mihiel and the Argonne Forest in which 1,500 allied aircraft participated, the army had no better perception about the future of the airplane than did the navy. During the war the automobile industry had retooled to build aircraft engines, but at the signing of the armistice the government cancelled all contracts for future delivery of airplanes. The fledgling aircraft industry in the United States quietly disbanded and quickly ceased to exist.

During the immediate postwar years, future strategy considerations came to dominate discussions. In foreign policy the choice boiled down either to some sort of alliances for mutual defenses and peacekeeping or isolationism in the Western Hemisphere. National military discussions revolved around a different set of concerns. Had the events of the First World War altered the basic concept of using a navy as the peacetime force to defend American shipping lanes around the world and of holding a skeleton army force to defend the mainland and act as a cadre to train a new army if future war became probable? The airplane, for example, could easily fit into any of the scenarios. Army officers such as William Mitchell and Henry Arnold, after seeing the role of aircraft in combat, argued for a strong air force to protect the mainland against any kind of enemy attack, including those by sea. A few officers in the navy saw the airplane as an offensive weapon which could extend the range and effectiveness of the fleet as it operated in enemy waters. Among those officers, Captain Thomas Craven and Admirals Bradley A. Fiske, William F. Fullum, and William S. Sims gave the greatest vocal support.

Events would soon occur that would alter what the navy had developed over thirty years. Neither sharp nor crisp, the ensuing debate at first obscured as much as it clarified; rather, the developing concepts of the nature of national security languished in the midst of the wrong debate over the wrong issue. Brigadier-General William Mitchell embarked upon the task of convincing the navy and Congress, which appropriated its funds, that the airplane, acting in a coastal defense capacity, could sink a battleship at sea. Mitchell, because he argued for the air defense of the mainland, fell easily into the hands of those who advocated isolationism. Those in the navy such as Admirals Sims, Fiske, and Fullum also argued for the role of the airplane, but they viewed it as an offensive weapon used by the fleet to assist in carrying American power and influence thousands of miles away from the mainland. In fact both groups had strong positions: the airplane could defend against the ship and could also operate in support of it. Naval officers recognized the dual role a battleship could play in carrying power against a remote enemy and by acting as a last line of defense in home waters against the enemy's ships, but they were slow to see a similar role for the airplane. Mitchell and other air advocates raised a threat to the navy with each call for more aircraft appropriations. In peacetime, dollars diverted toward research and development of aircraft and their eventual procurement could thwart the navy in its unchanging quest for the forty-eight-battleship fleet. Natural allies in the two services failed to act in unison on the airplane, and those entrenched groups such as the General Board and the Joint Board, opposed to increased air power, succeeded in pushing Congress to cut funds.

In the debate surrounding the League of Nations, the secretary of the navy argued that by defeating the treaty, the Senate would place greater pressure on the navy to build its fleet and accept the major responsibility of defending the country. There is evidence that both Great Britain and Japan assumed the United States government would increase its battle fleet if and when it rejected the treaty. Yet, as the navy sought to build ships for future security, it initially ignored the weapons system that could most logically support Mahan's dictates and its own avowed mission. For if, as Mitchell contended, coastal aircraft had the ability to sink capital ships approaching from distances of several miles offshore, the only way to combat this defensive weapon was to use air power in support of the fleet and neutralize the defensive air cover and hence restore the offensive value of the battleship. Shortly after the end of the war, the British and Japanese both began construction on carriers to use as offensive weapons and to provide air support for battle fleets. They assumed they could effectively carry the offense to distant areas. To the other naval powers it seemed obvious that the United States, given its geographical isolation, would do the same. Even though Great Britain had bases throughout Asia, it still had need of airpower on board ships to support its operations in Asia and the Pacific. Japan wanted aircraft carriers in order to convey its potential power throughout the Pacific and, if necessary, hold the United States at bay. Yet even with an airplane radius of approximately 200 miles of operational flight, the navy saw itself at no disadvantage against carriers as long as the planes stationed in the Philippines for coastal defense could operate.

Another ominous factor entered American naval planning in the immediate postwar period. According to Mahan, Great Britain had to have sea power and access to commerce routes if she hoped to remain a great power. Weakened by the war, the temptation to use an alliance to protect British commerce in areas where the Royal Navy could not project power might increase to the point that the Japanese would continue to look promising as an ally in the Pacific. During the early days of the First World War in Europe, the American navy had anxieties about British policies toward neutral ships such as those of the United States. When the British navy escorted neutral merchant vessels into British harbors for the process of visit and search, it became obvious to the Americans that Britain still ruled the waves. Coincidence or not, the General Board began its push for "a navy second to none" in 1915. After the war the navy did not relax its vigilance toward the British. In the fall of 1919, the General Board warned Secretary Daniels that Great Britain viewed the expansion of the American merchant marine with "jealousy and alarm." The board noted that "in every such case in the past Great Britain has resorted to war" in order to remove the threat.

Within Congress a heated debate raged regarding not only the League of Nations but also the military posture of the United States. The mobilization effort of the Great War seemed to have gone well enough, and many legislators and citizens believed if a future war came, Americans could secure success again by means similar to those used to mobilize and transport an armed force wherever necessary. That theory failed to account for the fact that the United States had almost two full years to prepare and to mobilize for munitions and war material production while being virtually untouched by the war. Nonetheless, if war had to come again, preparation would come in due course—as long as Americans had coastal defenses and a large navy to hold an enemy away while mobilization ran its course.

Republican Senator William E. Borah of Idaho, however, represented the thought that eventually prevailed in Congress. He saw armaments as the cause of war and viewed the reduction of war readiness as the best means of avoiding war. The senator, knowing the navy's predisposition toward battleships and hence large expenditures and visible armaments, inquired of the navy what ideal mix it wished between ships, aircraft, and submarines. The navy, of course, still held up the battleship as the mainstay of power. That response, as Borah had expected, allowed him to attack the expenditures for ships he called obsolete. Although not in a majority, an increasing number of officers in the army and navy believed in the airplane as the weapon of the future; they provided Borah and his supporters with all the quotations, testimony, and evidence they needed to mount a campaign against costly and, according to him, outdated weapons which had a mission they could not achieve in any event.

The debate over the role of air power in the navy continued despite the pronouncements that aircraft could neither greatly enhance the battle fleet nor, if used by an enemy against it, greatly hinder the fleet. In 1917 the British had successfully landed an airplane on a flight deck while the ship was under way and that led directly to a Royal Navy request for aircraft carriers. In turn, Admiral Sims, as commander of the United States Naval Forces in Europe, told the American navy of the Grand Fleet's desire for accompanying aircraft and advised that Americans needed to match the British decision. By late 1918 the

General Board decided to build an aircraft carrier by converting a collier, the *USS Jupiter*. The chief of Naval Operations, Admiral William S. Benson, countermanded the orders to convert the *Jupiter,* but Secretary Daniels overruled him, and the conversion process began in mid-1919. The debate over air power within the navy did not end, and, as an encounter with Billy Mitchell two years later would prove, the airplane would neither soon nor easily find acceptance as more than an extension and enhancement of the battle fleet.

In 1921 General Billy Mitchell got his chance to prove the value of the airplane at the expense of the battleship and hence to add to the argument by Senator Borah and others. In July the navy placed a German dreadnought of 27,000 tons in the Atlantic sixty miles off the coast of Virginia. Mitchell himself flew one of the planes that among them carried a total of six 1,000-pound bombs and seven 2,000-pound bombs. The first of the larger bombs sealed the fate of the ship; it sank twenty-one minutes later. The battleship, of course, had not fired back. The Joint Board of the Army and Navy declared that the test did not duplicate a warlike environment and discounted the results. The Joint Board then reconfirmed its support of the battleship as the main offensive force of the fleet and hence of American security.

The various debates within the military and in Congress had thus resulted in the reaffirmation of the Mahan doctrine regarding the role of the battleship even in the face of strong evidence to the contrary and despite the fact that other nations thought otherwise. As the world readjusted in the first few years after fighting the war to end all wars, the United States held to a national security strategy that did not differ from that of twenty years earlier. The submarine, the tank, the airplane, and a variety of repeating and high velocity arms had proved most important in the First World War. Yet American strategy and defense planning generally ignored the future implications of those weapons systems.

The lack of a defense strategy that accounted for current technology or at least accommodated the growing chorus of dissent within the army and navy gave the public and Congress the incentive to seek a different approach to national security. Most observers portray the interwar period as one in which the United States had no national security policy. In reality there were two national security policies. The military had a strategy that envisioned Japan as the potential enemy and viewed the fleet led by battleships as the best means of curtailing Japanese ambitions. A series of bases from Pearl Harbor to Manila Bay provided the support for the fleet and a barrier to further Japanese expansion. Growing in influence within the government and with the public was a countervailing thesis that argued if battleships were indeed the primary instruments of war, then the avoidance of war could come about by controlling or balancing the number of battleships. The Washington Conference and the others that followed it, attempted, in the eyes of those who held this second thesis, to remove the causes or at least limit the numbers of the primary weapons of war. The army and the navy had spent too much time in public debate and conveyed the impression that they had no security policy or even consensus on the nature and use of military power. By default, the control of national security moved from the military to another locus of power in Washington.

The disarmament, or more accurately arms control efforts, of the treaties limited the number of ships the United States could build or possess. Interservice and intraservice rivalry over the weapons of war, not over the strategy of a future war, marred the credibility of the military. The desire of the American people to get on with life and prosperity in the aftermath of a great war gave the military a decided disadvantage as it realized it must compete with the diplomats for congressional and public support.

A variety of factors contributed to the shift from military power to diplomacy as the peace-keeping mechanism of the United States government. Budget pressures caused congresses and presidents to apply care to military appropriations. Some degree of guilt or at least misgiving in Congress over the absence of American participation in the Versailles treaty and League of Nations may also have caused some uneasiness. The war had thrust the United States into a world leadership role. Great power status carried with it greater responsibility for mature national behavior. As public opinion and Congress slowly grasped the significance of that responsibility, America sought for ways to make the country more respectable to their world compatriots. In 1924 the Rogers Act established a professional Foreign Service intended to make American diplomats equal in ability to their counterparts in Europe. American trade and commerce became influential in Europe and signs emerged that the United States had backed away from its period of flirtation with imperialism. The nation eagerly turned to diplomacy as its security policy. The third decade of the century became, thus far, the only one in which the United States military found itself steadily overshadowed by the Department of State.

The military foundation for an "activist" foreign policy did not yet exist. While the United States had increased its presence and influence in world affairs since 1898, it had not proportionately enlarged militarily. From a pacifist perspective, that was good. For if arms and men were not immediately available in large quantities, the extent of government activities overseas would tend to be restricted, perhaps preventing full American participation in foreign events that might turn into "quagmires" causing high losses of men and money. In the pacifist view, as many arms and men as were available would in fact be used.

From the viewpoint of the Department of War, the problem was not that simple, although a somewhat similar solution was reached. While recognizing the larger American world role, the War Department could not help but remember the traditional reluctance of Congress to vote funds for the army in peacetime. American commitments abroad not only might overextend the capacity of the army to react in support of administration foreign policy, but, even worse, could place the army in a dangerous military situation not of its own choosing. The use of the navy and the marines on a small scale in both Latin America and East Asia had not, with the exception of the Philippine insurrection from 1900 to 1905, placed the army in difficulty. The Philippine insurrection was, however, exactly the type of situation that the army wished to avoid. It became torn between its duty to meet obligations in support of American foreign policies and its lack of men and supplies. Convinced, on the basis of past experiences, that it was going to receive neither of the latter, the army developed isolationist strategies not totally abandoned even during the Second World War. Defense of the continent fell within the army's limited purview and gave parameters to its ambitions. As a result, except for the draft in 1917–1918, the United States did not have sufficient military manpower to carry out anything but an isolationist foreign policy.

American military reformers wrestled with these problems, and in 1920 one notable attempt was made at a solution when a proposal for Universal Military Training was discussed for the National Defense Act of that year. Knowing that the World War I army would be broken up and would probably revert to its prewar size and status, men like young Lieutenant Colonel John McAuley Palmer developed a plan. Rather than hopelessly calling for a large professional army based on regular army officers, the plan supported by the higher-ups, Palmer called for a small regular army that would be supplemented, in times of need, by already trained citizen soldiers. Supported by General Pershing, who had been impressed by the quality of conscripted American soldiers fighting in France, Palmer courageously stated that "the War Department bill proposes incomplete preparedness at excessive cost and under forms that are not in harmony with the genius of American institutions." Fearful of an army that did not have widespread public support, he hoped with UMT to "build military strength into the democratic state without creating an exclusive samurai caste." We must, he said, "have military power without militarism." A citizen's army would also be more reluctant, he believed, to embark on imperial adventures.

Military planners hypothesized that any future war would be dealt with by conscription. The regular army was viewed as a compact force in readiness that could receive and train citizen soldiers during rapid mobilization. This approach contributed to a unique situation described by Samuel Huntington as a conspicuous absence of the "Glorification of War" by the American military. As he noted in his study of the American military, during the crisis of the 1930s, military leaders often urged diplomats to behave with caution because of weakness of the national security establishment.

Palmer and his supporters failed in their quest in 1920 because they underestimated the political power of the individual state National Guard units, whose status UMT appeared to threaten. The seeds, however, had been planted, and Palmer, strongly backed by a young colleague from the 1920 struggle, George C. Marshall, would seek a similar goal in 1944. Nevertheless, from 1920 until 1940 and the passage of Selective Service, the American army had neither the men nor the equipment to be an instrument of American foreign policy.

As the military establishment quarreled within itself about the efficacy of the weapons systems and as it demonstrated its lack of cohesiveness and conceptualization in national security policy, the nation happily sped toward normalcy and complacency. Military budgets declined, but Congress often appropriated money for projects the army or navy had not requested, such as research on aircraft and use of air power with the fleet.

The plethora of peace initiatives and conferences in the decade of the 1920s left the leadership and responsibility for national security in the Department of State. The military first had to resolve its own internal disputes. In 1920, the Army Air Service, created and made independent from the Signal Corps, came into existence. That year, the budget for aviation research in the army reached $4 1/2 million. Although the navy had disbanded the Office of Naval Aviation in 1919, Congress established the Bureau of Aeronautics for the navy in 1921. The first aircraft carrier, the converted *USS Langley,* joined the fleet in early 1922. Both services began to pay greater attention to the use of aviation by the military forces of other countries. Billy Mitchell, making himself a sacrifice to the cause he held so strongly, preached air power so openly that a court-martial became the only alternative for the army. But young army and navy officers volunteered in increasing numbers to take flight training and one of the first three trained army pilots, Henry (Hap) Arnold, campaigned for air power as he steadily moved upward through the ranks. The naval conferences of Washington and London forced many young naval officers to reevaluate their careers as they saw command opportunities grow more limited.

In all of this, security planning and strategic doctrine remained constant. The Japanese, in the war planning, retained their status as the most likely opponent. Britain and perhaps other European countries with interests in East Asia would probably provide some assistance in the event of war. The plan for waging war with the Japanese, code named "Orange," identified the Philippines once again as the key to withstanding Japanese thrusts to the south. By 1930, the navy, still reevaluating the demonstration of air power by Billy Mitchell, now thought of the airplane as a vital component of the defense of the Philippine Islands. The Orange Plan, however, retained the battleship fleet as the mainstay of the American defense of the Pacific. The airplane would protect the fleet at anchor and provide advance notice of enemy fleet movements toward American bases. Plans for the forty-eight-battleship fleet did not flourish following the Washington Conference. Congress, in fact, did not even vote enough funds to allow the navy to build up to the full strength permitted by the treaty. By 1928 it had come close, but because of the Great Depression a year later, shipbuilding never reached levels consistent with navy planning or the requirements of the Orange Plan. The army had a postwar force level of 280,000 men, but after 1929, budget constraints caused a reduction to 145,000 troops. In 1925 the Army Air Service had 1,436 aircraft of which two-thirds were obsolete. In 1926 Congress approved a building plan intended to provide 400 new planes a year. Yet a decade later the service had only 1,247 total aircraft.

Two factors caused the military to fall below its desired force levels. Internal dissention, indecision, and budget problems brought forth both by the normalization following the war and later by the depression created serious complications for planners. During the decade, the lack of battleships in sufficient numbers caused some revision of strategic planning and operations. It also led to a more serious examination of the role of the airplane, flown from ship and shore, as a less costly and more available offensive weapon. Given the minimal role of the battleship in the Second World War, one could argue that the United States lost nothing by being unable to meet its battle fleet force structure in the interwar years and, in fact, may have been better off by having to diversify in its offensive systems. Faced with choices imposed upon it by the naval conferences, the navy had to change its force structure and planning for the use of national power. Throughout the decade following the war the guiding principles for national security in the military remained Mahan's. By 1931, when the United States government found itself unable to thwart Japanese adventurism in East Asia, American

Colonel William Mitchell at his court martial, 1925.

military planners had already made serious reevaluations of power concepts and strategy.

The navy had requested and received two ships (both, incidentally, constructed in uncompleted, unscrapped hulls from the 1916 program not destroyed by the Washington treaty), designed and built as aircraft carriers, the *USS Saratoga,* commissioned in 1927, and the *USS Lexington* in 1928. In its very first war game exercise in 1929, the *Saratoga* swung away from the main fleet and launched a mock air strike against the locks of the Panama Canal. It came as a complete surprise to the defenders; the referees for the war game declared the locks destroyed and the attacking fleet the winner. Fleet Problem Number Nine, the *Saratoga* mock attack, had an enormous impact on naval strategy in the next decade. Admiral William A. Moffett, appointed the chief of the Bureau of Aeronautics in the navy, led the effort to integrate the carrier into the battle fleet. Naval conference restrictions that forbade the enlargement of American naval and air bases west of Hawaii facilitated his task. If airplanes had the ability to play a major military role in the western Pacific, carriers would have to take the place of island airfields. While the battleship would remain the chief capital ship of the United States Navy until Pearl Harbor, the aircraft carrier would, by then, be well enough accepted and integrated by the navy to play the decisive military role for the navy in the Pacific.

Thus while the world had changed rapidly, in both a political and technological sense, American national security policy remained static but, as indicated, perhaps less static than many at the time might have believed. Nevertheless, neither American diplomacy nor the American military could face the future with complete confidence. The challenge of new nations and the vision of new leaders with new ideas brought unforeseen complications. These challenges first became prominent during the presidency of Franklin D. Roosevelt.

Selected Reading

Stephen E. Ambrose and James A. Barber, eds., offer an important series of essays on the *Military and American Society* (1972). Two sociological works are most interesting: Morris Janowitz' *The Professional Soldier: A Social and Political Portrait* (1960) and Peter Karsten's *The Naval Aristocracy: The Golden*

Age of Annapolis and the Emergence of Modern American Navalism (1972). The structure in this period can best be sought in Paul Y. Hammond's *Organizing for Defense: The American Military Establishment in the Twentieth Century* (1961). Bernard Brodie's *War and Politics* (1973) is stimulating, while Richard Hobbes's *The Myth of Victory: What is Victory in War?* (1979) is questioning and provocative. Russell F. Weigley's *Towards an American Army: Military Thought From Washington to Marshall* (1962) deals with military organization.

The development of air power in the U.S. Navy is well documented in a book by Charles M. Melhorn, *Two-Block Fox: The Rise of the Aircraft Carrier, 1911–1929* (1974). Harold and Margaret Sprout's *Toward a New Order of Sea Power: American Naval Policy and the World Scene, 1918–1922* (1940) is a useful introduction, as is Gerald E. Wheeler's *Prelude to Pearl Harbor: The United States Navy and the Far East, 1921–1931* (1963). The United States Air Force Academy publishes a series of *Harmon Memorial Lectures* in monograph form. Those issues include: Number 21 by Noel Parrish entitled "The Influence of Air Power Upon Historians"; Michael Howard's lecture, Number 9, entitled "Strategy and Policy in 20th Century Warfare"; and Number 11 by Elting E. Morison, "The War of Ideas: The United States Navy, 1870–1890." Louis A. Sigaud's *Air Power and Unification: Douhet's Principles of Warfare and their Application to the United States* (1949) makes interesting reading today. H.H. "Hap" Arnold wrote a personal account of the development of the Air Force in a book entitled *Global Mission* (1949).

Army happenings are best found in I.B. Holley, Jr., *General John M. Palmer: Citizen Soldiers, and the Army of a Democracy* (1985) and Peter Karsten's *The Military in America: From the Colonial Era to the Present* (1980).

See also the military books in Chapter 1.

6 FDR and Isolationism

In March 1933 a remarkable man, known in the more polite Republican journals as "that man in the White House," became president of the United States. Franklin D. Roosevelt served an unprecedented twelve years until his death in 1945. Who can doubt Roosevelt's claim to the title of "American Politician *par excellance,*" the all-time American political champ? Unlike Wilson, FDR had the love and affection of the American people; his air of confidence and belief that a solution existed for every problem earned him a trust and devotion unparalleled in American history. Like Wilson's New Freedom, Roosevelt's domestic program, the New Deal, achieved success. Roosevelt's domestic problems, however, were of a far more serious nature than Wilson's and acted as a strong restraint on his conduct of foreign policy. Solving the Great Depression came first, and not until roughly 1937 did FDR begin to turn in a major way to foreign affairs. Cautious, if not overcautious, he refused to gamble his hard-earned political capital on risky overseas involvements. Roosevelt, as guilty of appeasement in the 1930s as Prime Minister Neville Chamberlain in Great Britain, escaped similar censure. Boldness, decisive leadership, and imagination did not mark FDR's foreign policies until his domestic consensus broke down over the Supreme Court struggle and he won the election of 1940. Only then did the "real" Roosevelt step forth. And, as with Wilson, deep controversy surrounds his actions, not only in what he actually did, but also in what he believed.

Historians face serious obstacles in dealing with FDR's conduct of foreign policy. First, Roosevelt directed foreign policy exactly as he **113** did domestic policy—crisis oriented, administratively unstructured, and outside of regular diplomatic channels. The crucial ultimate control of foreign policy, however, as it did with Wilson, rested in the president's hands. Second, he was the most consummate actor who ever lived in the White House, a chameleon who had made a career of appearing all things to all men, and few, if any, could claim they knew the genuine FDR. He often expressed startlingly different opinions on the same subject, even on the same day, to separate people. Roosevelt never viewed transparency of intentions and consistency of beliefs as important virtues. He liked to keep the broad picture to himself and reveal only bits and pieces to others. Third, added to these attributes there was a devious strain, for Roosevelt preferred to go around barriers and problems rather than meet them head-on, and that makes it even more difficult to comprehend his beliefs. And finally, there are the historical records themselves. FDR, unlike his cousin Theodore, wrote no revealing books and few letters, preferred to use the telephone or personal talks, and the result is that few records exist for much of what he said or did. Almost all of what historians know about Roosevelt's private beliefs come not from the president or official records, but from reports of those who dealt with him. Each, of course, may or may not have correctly reported the president's words. Also, a great many primary sources have either disappeared, were never made in the first place, or remain unavailable or obscured in foreign collections.

Roosevelt, in the words of James MacGregor Burns, certainly stands, like Wilson, as "fundamentally an idealist." He wanted a world of peace in which man, decent and moral, progressed toward bringing order out of chaos. Roosevelt never doubted man's advancement toward that goal or the possibility of solutions to man's problems. One finds few major differences, with the exception of the place of religion, between the goals sought by Wilson and those of Franklin Roosevelt; both stood squarely in the mainstream of the American liberal, idealist tradition. A master at reaching for immediate, achievable goals through any means possible, Roosevelt, unlike Wilson, did not always keep in mind the ultimate goal. In daily tactics, he was magnificient; but in grand strategy, his ability to use all available means to secure his goal, and not let the means justify the ends, he was less than magnificent. The president too often flew by the seat of his pants, depending on timing, intuition, and luck to carry him through foreign affairs as they had so well in domestic affairs. In short, he often had no plans beyond solving the immediate problem facing him.

It is time also to qualify the traditional portrait of Roosevelt as the happy warrior, cautiously but victoriously leading his troops against isolationist hordes. Historian Wayne Cole writes that "Roosevelt skillfully and almost ruthlessly demolished the isolationists and isolationism. . . . [and] with his triumph over the isolationists there was no turning back either for America or the world." Few would disagree that American participation in world affairs operated at a much higher level after 1945 than it did during the 1930s. Two points, however, remain of interest. Roosevelt did not fight the isolationists during most of the 1930s and came close to being one himself. He only openly parted from them in 1941 and did not seek to crush them until he had power, as well as the courage, to do so.

More important, did he not crush the isolationists too completely? Were there not elements of wisdom in their position? Isolationism has come to have pejorative overtones in its use and meaning. But, again, what did isolationists actually believe? They wanted to continue the traditional American freedom of action, unbound by any alliance or world organization. As each international incident arose, they wanted Americans to decide, at that time and not before, without the complication of precommitments of any kind, what would benefit the United States. Isolationists believed that Americans could best serve as an example of democracy and should not export democracy abroad through interventions and war. Such activities, in their opinion, would threaten, not defend, the very American values they purported to cherish at home. Isolationists feared that a presidential-military-industrial complex (although they did not use that term) might develop and lead to imperial adventures. It is also important to remember that American isolationism remained more selective than inclusive; disengagement from Europe did not conflict with a desire to control the Western Hemisphere or even push across the Pacific. In other words, many isolationists harkened back to the certain diplomatic tradition. In the post–Watergate-Vietnam era, it is possible to argue that their ideas and voice of restraint had a proper role to play. Had they continued to argue their ideas after 1945, perhaps their opposition might well have tempered some of the excesses of American foreign policy.

On whom did Roosevelt rely for his conduct of foreign policy? Cordell Hull was his secretary of state until 1944. While the president had great respect for the domestic political abilities of Hull, a long-time member of Congress and an expert on the tariff, he ignored Hull's advice on diplomatic affairs, kept the secretary uninformed and, on occasion, pulled the rug out from under Hull. Roosevelt essentially distrusted the Department of State and did not use it unless absolutely necessary; he did, however, often depend on the advice of Undersecretary Sumner Welles. That particular action did not contribute to a lasting friendship between Hull and Welles. FDR, like Wilson before him, also preferred to use personal diplomatic agents, such as Harry Hopkins and Patrick J. Hurley. When push came to shove, the president was his own secretary of state. But in Roosevelt's unstructured administrative model, however, this allowed not only Congress, as we shall describe shortly, but other executive departments, in particular the Treasury, to participate in the conduct of foreign policy.

Competition existed not only between different departments but within each of the bureaucratic structures. Each organization wanted to enhance its position against its opposition; the Department of State, for example, fought to prevent encroachments from Secretary of the Treasury Henry Morgenthau's international economic and financial experts. Each department had its own set of operating procedures and programs, developed over years, which led it to a certain type of thinking and conclusions. Finally, within each organization there were players whose interests were not only to protect their own department's turf but their own individual piece of that action within the department. They might represent a group or just their own view. We have already noted the arguments within the navy over the importance of aircraft, which brought both informal groups and diverse individuals to the forefront. In other words, politics played its role in presenting the various options. Some organizations and people were locked into positions that might or might not reflect the total national interest so much as their organizational and individual view that stressed more parochial interest. The openness and flexibility of the Roosevelt administrative style had its strengths, but the lack of central direction also weakened the overall approach of the government.

During his first term in office Roosevelt followed a policy of economic nationalism. Far more interested in restoring the economy of the United States than in helping to restore the world economy, FDR had to make a choice and chose the course that he felt would most likely benefit the country. This policy of Roosevelt's is best illustrated by the London Economic Conference of 1933. Some sixty-three nations gathered in London in an attempt to break down the high tariff barriers and establish an international stabilization of the currency by making foreign currencies freely interchangeable. Secretary Hull went to the conference with his program of tariff reciprocity. FDR, however, dropped his famous bombshell when he wired Hull to oppose tariff reduction and currency stabilization; the president feared such actions might endanger his New Deal program. This unfortunate move did not differ greatly from those economic policies which his Republican predecessors had followed.

During FDR's first term the United States government finally recognized the government of the Soviet Union. The Wilson administration had withheld recognition from the Soviet Union after 1917 because the U.S.S.R. had refused to pay Americans for property destroyed during the revolution; the Soviets also refused to recognize the validity of international agreements. And, of course, the American government assumed that when the Soviets called for the overthrow of capitalist governments, they probably meant the American government. But by 1933 Stalin had adopted the theory of "socialism in one country," and Russia also appeared more traditional and less revolutionary when it joined the League of Nations.

American businessmen played an important part in bringing about Soviet recognition when they expressed a desire to expand trade with the Soviet Union. General Electric, DuPont, Ford, and other American companies had already poured millions of dollars worth of industrial equipment into the Soviet Union in the late 1920s. When the Great Depression set in, hopes rose that recognition of the Soviet Union would open new markets. One writer wrote in the *New York Times* that "$500,000,000 of Russian orders would immediately appear on the desks of American industry" if the Soviet Union were recognized.

Roosevelt in October 1933 wrote the Soviet government and proposed negotiations about a resumption of relations. Maxim Litvinov, the Soviet Commissar of Foreign Affairs, came to Washington to conduct the talks. The Soviets hoped, in part, that recognition might lead to some common policy which the two powers could take against the Japanese encroachments in Manchuria. An exchange of notes then took place between Litvinov and Hull and Roosevelt: the Soviet Union promised that it would not interfere in American internal affairs, that it would not support communist subversive organizations in the United States agitating against the American government, that it would grant religious liberty to Americans in Russia and give them a fair trial if accused of crimes, and that it would negotiate a settlement of the debts. With this understanding, the Roosevelt administration recognized the Soviet Union in November 1933.

What were the results? The Soviet Union failed to keep any of its promises. On the key question of debts, it began to push counterclaims for American intervention in Russia from 1918 to 1920. The expected boom in trade never came. Instead of fostering cooperation and friendship, recognition sharpened distrust and hostility. By 1939, with the signing of the Nazi-Soviet Pact, any American sympathy for the Soviet Union had disappeared in the United States. Recognition did not immediately help the United States in its relations with the Soviet Union, but, on balance, neither had the previous policy of nonrecognition. Once the United States had made the initial mistake of failing to recognize a *de facto* regime, it became difficult to develop a feeling of mutual trust.

The economic chaos that swept through the United States and Europe shortly before and during the Roosevelt administration had an immediate and broad impact upon foreign policy and military preparedness. Not all of the victims of the economic collapse behaved in the same manner. While Germany took an aberrant course under Adolf Hitler, for the most part, the democracies turned their attention toward the needs of their citizens. Regimes in Germany, Italy, Japan, and the Soviet Union created fear among their neighbors. The behavior of these countries earned the label of totalitarian as they subordinated the needs of citizens to those of the state as defined by highly authoritarian leaders. Armaments were not sacrificed for the needs of the civilian population, and in all cases, the ability of the people to thwart the will of their leaders was greatly limited. The democracies were at a disadvantage. Yet, the bellicose behavior of Hitler in Europe caused European countries to insist on a reasonable level of security and the armaments that were needed to provide that security. Following on the heels of the decade of disarmament conferences and renewed hope that war had indeed been outlawed, the United States did less than its fellow democracies in Europe to prepare for potential attempts at intimidation by Hitler and other authoritarian leaders.

The United States Navy had never reached its treaty strength, although in the period just prior to the collapse of the stock market it had come close. As the depression worsened and lengthened, the Navy Board realized it would need to adjust planning to its reduced capabilities. This readjustment process came as the navy continued to cope with its internal debate over the merits of the airplane in naval strategy and force requirements. By 1930 the aircraft carrier had become a viable part of the fleet, although not all naval flag officers were enamoured of the new weapon and its impact on strategy and doctrine. Billy Mitchell had demonstrated the vulnerability of a capital ship when attacked by aircraft. Fleet exercises had demonstrated the value of the carrier in an offensive situation. The navy had long believed in the airplane as a defensive and reconnaissance arm of the fleet but remained reluctant to risk a building program of aircraft and carriers in exchange for battleships.

For a decade after the Great War the airplane developed in speed and range as well as in the capacity to carry heavier loads. Congress had sufficient faith in the ability of the airplane and the reliability of its performance to grant air carriers the right to carry mail. Although the frontier of flight had steadily been pushed outward, the flight by Charles Lindbergh from the United States to the continent of Europe in 1927 had proved that an airplane could operate at ranges sufficient to challenge the navy in its role of taking the battle to the enemy. Mitchell continued to write and speak in behalf of the airplane as the weapon of most strategic importance to the United States. As technology developed, his advocacy became more widely believable. Yet, if there was a revolution within the armed forces about the airplane, it was a very quiet one.

The three Republican administrations following the Great War had placed their emphasis upon arms negotiations, limitations on shipbuilding, and the efficacy of the diplomatic corps. The first two administrations had other options; the third probably did not. By the time the ill-fated Hoover administration took office, domestic issues blocked many of the options that previously had existed. Whether the military faced good times or bad times, it remained preoccupied with the belief that Japan would be the potential adversary and the objective was to protect shipping and supply lines to the farthermost American outpost, the Philippines. In 1931 Mitchell wrote in *Liberty Magazine* about the United States being "one of the most warlike great nations on earth" and yet one of the "least prepared" for war. Mitchell, whose fame continued to grow following his death shortly before the beginning of World War II, predicted in a report prior to his court-martial, and in articles following it, that the Japanese would attack the American fleet in the Pacific by surprise. He even predicted the attack would come at Pearl Harbor in the early morning. The Mitchell mystic would last a long time thanks to such a prediction, but nothing about his suggestion of the Japanese as a potential aggressor was surprising, even to his more avid detractors.

As the leadership passed from the Republicans to the Democrats in 1933, the depression continued to worsen. The agenda for President Franklin Roosevelt was clearly domestic recovery, not foreign affairs. There was an insufficient flow of money to allow for the building of the military or even the maintenance of existing forces. Issues of national security and military preparation had to take a low priority in the eyes of the administration.

The navy was particularly aggrieved about the curtailment of its building program. Its ability to conduct the mission assigned to it depended upon a fleet, and a large one at that. Funding limitations had dictated that there would be no major naval base beyond the Hawaiian Islands. A battle fleet capable of carrying the offense throughout the Pacific and simultaneously capable of defending sea lanes to the Philippine Islands was a necessity. The navy did not have such a fleet, and construction toward it lagged more each year. The army, which had peacetime limits of 280,000 men since 1921, fell through attrition and failure of adequate funding to the level of 145,000 during the early years of the Great Depression. The air corps was funded in direct proportion to the size of the army and therefore suffered the same decline as did ground forces. Receipts to the national government declined from 1931 through 1934, while expenditures almost doubled. Between 1930 and 1936, the national debt doubled from $16.8 billion to $33.8 billion.

National security planning was in disarray during the years of greatest financial strain on the national budget. The depression, however, was not the true cause of the lack of a national security posture in the decade when it was to be most needed. In the years immediately following the First World War, all the administrations had opted for security through arms control and diplomacy rather than by means of military force. The navy especially and to a lesser degree the army and air corps were placed in a secondary role in the conduct of security affairs. The optimism of the decade of arms limitations reached its height with the Kellogg-Briand Pact. Soon thereafter, military considerations began to loom larger as world affairs raised questions about arms control.

Serious events occurred in both East Asia and Europe, and they slowly but surely demanded first attention and then action. The Japanese had annexed Korea in 1910. In the intervening years the Japanese had started to move north, across the Yalu River, and to expand their interests in the three northeastern provinces of China collectively called Manchuria. But in 1931 the Japanese finally ran into the rising tide of Chinese nationalism. Chiang Kai-shek hoped to recover all of China's former provinces from various warlords and to include those territories in a unified Chinese state. Diplomatic negotiations between the two nations had failed. On September 18, 1931, the Japanese army began to occupy the Manchurian city of Mukden on the South Manchurian Railroad; the railroad zone was the only area into which the Japanese had a treaty right to send troops. The Japanese accused the Chinese of exploding a bomb along the railroad.

President Hoover's secretary of state, Henry Stimson, had pursued a policy of watchful waiting, while the Chinese appealed to the League of Nations that Japan had broken the League covenant; they also com-

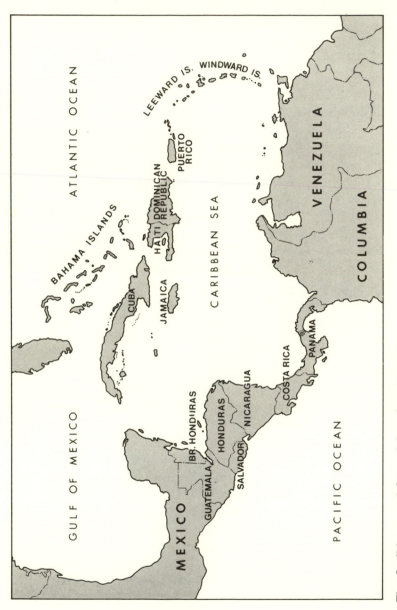

The Caribbean and Central America, 1914–1945

plained to the United States government that the Japanese had broken the Kellogg-Briand Pact by resorting to war. Stimson believed, quite correctly, that the Japanese army had acted without the consent of the Japanese government. He hoped that the Japanese foreign minister would influence the government to call the troops back. But as time went by, Japanese troops expanded over the entire province. The question went before the League council, with an American representative present, and a League resolution calling for the withdrawal of Japanese troops met defeat by a Japanese veto; however, a resolution authorizing an international commission to investigate the dispute was passed. Even Stimson became convinced that the Japanese government could not restrain the militarists.

From 1931 to 1933 President Hoover and Secretary Stimson, largely through words, attempted to halt Japanese aggression and, if possible, to bring about the return of Manchuria to China, but Stimson soon had to label this policy a failure. Personally he would have welcomed economic sanctions by the League and American cooperation in their enforcement, but the president strongly opposed any action that might involve the United States in a war. The Hoover administration did attempt to bluff the Japanese by sending naval vessels to Shanghai to protect American lives and property, and by holding the American fleet at Pearl Harbor in a state of readiness.

Perhaps the most important step taken by Stimson was the announcement of the Stimson Non-recognition Doctrine on January 7, 1932. This was really a resurrection of an old Wilson-Bryan idea of 1915 protesting the Twenty-One Demands of the Japanese on China. Stimson notified the Japanese government that the United States "cannot admit the legality of any situation *de facto* nor does it intend to recognize any treaty or agreement . . . which may impair the treaty rights of the United States or its citizens in China. . . . or recognize any situation, treaty or agreement which may be brought about by means contrary . . . to the Pact of Paris." He asked other signatories of the Nine-Power Treaty of 1921 to send similar warnings. The British, however, more than aware of the Japanese danger, did not act, preferring that the Japanese stay in Manchuria rather than cast eyes on areas to the south that included strong British interests. The Japanese government replied that it certainly intended to live up to any treaty it had signed.

Stimson then tried to create a diplomatic stir by writing an open letter to Senator William E. Borah of the Senate Foreign Relations Committee. The letter reviewed the American policy of the Open Door, the Nine-Power Treaty, and the Pact of Paris and concluded that the United States saw no reason to abandon any principles which it had accepted in those treaties. Stimson hinted that if the Japanese persisted on their path of aggression, the Hoover administration would leave the Five-Power Treaty and begin to build up its fleet and fortify its Pacific Islands.

Both the nonrecognition doctrine and the Borah letter relied on attempts to stir up world public opinion against the Japanese, but American and world opinion, largely occupied by the depression, could not and did not stop the Japanese advance. Both American attempts did indicate the growing friction between the two governments of Japan and the United States. The American dependence on moral weapons to stop the Japanese failed, but Roosevelt's first administration continued exactly the same policies.

The League of Nations sent a commission to Manchuria in the summer of 1932. The commission produced the famous review of Manchurian conditions known as the Lytton Report. While critical of the Japanese, the report did not propose a return to conditions existing before the Japanese attack; rather, it recommended a new treaty, which would safeguard the interests of Japan after the withdrawal of both Japanese and Chinese troops. In other words it gave support to Chinese sovereignty but also had provisions to protect Japan's economic interests. But the Japanese rejected what to the American government seemed a satisfactory statement. In September 1932 the Japanese created the puppet regime of Manchukuo which League members refused to recognize. The Japanese government then gave the required two-years' notice that the Japanese would not renew the naval clauses of the Washington and London treaties when they expired in 1936. Japanese actions certainly weakened the League and also indicated a breakdown in the East Asian peace structure created at the Washington Conference.

At the same time, challenges to the Versailles settlement by the Germans and the Italians created threats to the parallel European structure, although the danger of Hilter was not clear to all at that time. Harold Laski in Great Britain wrote in November 1932 that "The day when they [the Nazis] were a vital threat is gone. . . . It is not unlikely that Hitler will end his career as an old man in some Bavarian village who, in the biergarten in the evening, tells his intimates how he nearly overturned the German Reich." Two American historians, however, writing almost fifty years later, argued that "Adolf Hitler was a child—a misbegotten child of World War I—an unacknowledged offspring of Woodrow Wilson's humanitarianism and idealism. If the American President had not involved the United States in the war of 1917, Europe would have continued to make a peace of exhaustion in its own way, as it had for centuries past." Perhaps somewhere in between a mistaken judgment and hindsight lies the pragmatic truth. Most Americans, and their president, either did not see a threat, assumed they could ignore the rest of the world without serious consequences, or concluded they could not stop the Europeans from warring against each other.

In the early 1930s the United States did seem in the grip of an isolationist fever which took almost a decade to break. Disillusionment with the results of the First World War, as mentioned previously, certainly played a major part in the development of isolationism. Wilson's world "made safe for democracy" did not exist, and the resultant reaction contributed not only to the growth of isolationism but reinforced old prewar feelings about the essential wickedness of warlike Europeans. The Allies had tricked Americans into the First World War to further their aims. The appearance of revisionist books such as Walter Millis' *Road to War* in 1934, which suggested that the United States had indeed entered the war to further Allied selfish desires, added to this belief. Resentment that the Allies had not paid back their war debts also fueled the fires. "Once bitten, twice shy" went an old folk saying, and Americans had apparently decided against taking a chance on a second bite.

Congress appointed a Munitions Investigation Committee in 1934 to inquire into charges raised by books such as *Merchants of Death,* by Helmuth Englebrecht, which contended that American munitions makers had conspired to take the United States into the war in order to make more profits and to save the Europeans who owed them so much money. Senator Gerald Nye, a Republican isolationist from North Dakota, headed the committee, and for two years its sensational hearings were headlined in almost every newspaper. Nye's committee findings were meager; its investigation simply could not prove that the munitions industry had influenced the United States government to enter the First World War. Few Americans actually read the report, but many remembered the charges. As often happened, Americans looked for simple explanations, and politicans gave them.

Congress then got down to business; if the president would not protect the United States from such disasters, Congress would. The first step, passage of the Johnson Debt Default Act of 1934, prohibited loans to any country behind on its payments or which had failed to pay at all on the First World War loans. The act also banned the future sale of any foreign securities in the American market by these countries. After the bill was passed even those nations making payments of one sort or another defaulted, and it is possible, though not probable, that the American stance may have convinced the British and the French of the difficulty of taking any stand against Mussolini or Hitler since the Americans would give them neither political nor ongoing financial support.

In 1933 Germany withdrew from the League of Nations. In March of 1933 Hitler announced compulsory military training and increased his army to 500,000 men, a level forbidden by the Treaty of Versailles. Then in 1936 Hitler specifically repudiated the Treaty of Versailles and proceeded to occupy the Rhineland. And last, but far from least, in October 1935 Mussolini had invaded Ethiopia.

The League of Nations declared Italy an aggressor and asked members to impose economic sanctions. The list of prohibited articles, however, did not include oil, iron and steel, coal and coke; these, of course, are the major materials of modern war. The main reason given for their omission? The Italians could acquire these materials from a non-League country such as the United States which did not have an embargo on those items.

The American peace movement of the 1930s, rooted in the experiences of the First World War, contributed to the debate over neutrality. To be sure, peace societies began in the United States early in the nineteenth century, but these groups did not have the widespread public support or the influence on policy formulation that peace organizations would come to command during the interwar period. The effects of World War I cannot be minimized in explaining this phenomena. Disillusioned by the horror of global conflict, and unsatisfied by a peace that did little to alter the causes of that conflict, a generation of Americans sought an alternative to international unrest.

Throughout the 1920s peace organizations found increasing support among Americans, and pursued programs in support of disarmament, international organization, development of an international legal system, and international economic cooperation, in the belief that worldwide cooperation would lead to worldwide harmony. By the end of the decade, the peace movement flourished.

Before considering the role that the movement played in the American society prior to World War II, it is important to examine its composition and appeal. By 1930 the peace movement consisted of a complex network of diverse organizations. Each had its own agenda and constituency. Some represented a specific social strata, such as the religious and women's organizations. Others favored a distinct functional program—lobbying, for example, or representation of a specific issue, such as opposition to ROTC. A 1933 study conducted by the Commission for Coordination of Efforts for Peace identified 12 international, 28 national, and 37 local peace societies operating in the United States. In addition to these, a large number of organizations not directly involved in peace work but maintaining some relationship to the peace effort existed.

In an attempt to facilitate our understanding of the peace movement as a whole, Charles Chatfield, the leading historian of the interwar peace movement, divides the peace societies into three distinct groups: radicals, conservative internationalists, and pacifists. Radical organizations were on the extreme left of the political spectrum, and fell largely under communist domination. The American League Against War and Fascism, for example, began as a coalition of left wing and pacifist groups, and advocated a united front against war. As communist influence within the group increased, other elements of the coalition exited the united front. Other pacifist groups remained wary of the radicals throughout the decade, isolating radical organizations from the mainstream of the peace movement. The radicals believed that war was symptomatic of the capitalist system, and they were especially active in attempts to organize American youth in the cause of peace.

The conservative internationalists were committed to international cooperation, and they favored the development of an international legal and organizational system. They were also supporters of international economic cooperation. Chatfield includes groups such as the Carnegie Endowment for International Peace, the League of Nations Association, and the World Peace Foundation in the conservative internationalist camp. They were particularly concerned with educating the public on international affairs. Because the leaders of these organizations were often influential in government circles, they sought to influence policy makers informally toward the cause of peace.

Chatfield's third group consists of pacifist organizations. Formed during and after World War I, pacifist societies repudiated war completely and combined their activism for peace with support for social reform. There were a great many pacifist organizations, such as the Fellowship for Reconciliation, the National Council for Prevention of War, and the Women's International League for Peace and Freedom. But these groups had a small and often overlapping membership. It has been estimated that the core of full-time workers within pacifist societies numbered no more than a hundred. Pacifist groups were, nonetheless, extremely vocal and were successful in focusing public attention on issues they considered important. Unlike the internationalists, pacifists attempted to influence policy formulation directly by bringing public pressure to bear upon government.

With the exception of the radicals, the organizations within the peace movement were all loosely related to one another because they had, to a certain extent, overlapping constituencies, leaders, and goals. Taken alone, none could mount sufficient pressure to influence policy directly. By unifying around those issues that were not divisive, however, peace organizations were able to exert an influence entirely disproportionate to their size. The failure of the Geneva Conference of Disarmament to produce concrete results, and the rapid deterioration of international harmony lent a sense of urgency to the campaign for peace. The Senate's refusal to sanction American entrance into the World Court gave added impetus to a joint effort between pacifists and internationalists. Thus throughout the 1930s the pacifist and internationalist wings of the peace movement aligned and realigned in search of an effective coalition.

These attempts at coalition, however, rested on a shaky foundation. Although the two groups were united in seeking peace, they were divided over basic principles and approaches. At the beginning of the decade pacifists shared the faith of internationalists in the ability of collective security to promote peace. The failure of the League of Nations effectively to counter Japanese incursions into Manchuria in 1931 left many pacifists disillusioned. They came to regard collective security as an agency by which great powers acted in their own interests to preserve the status quo. Consequently pacifists came to view mandatory neutrality as the only effective measure to keep the United States out of war.

The 1935 battle for neutrality brought this fundamental difference in principle to light at the same time that the peace groups were making moves toward coalition. Both internationalists and pacifists were committed to some form of neutrality, but they could not agree on what form neutrality legislation should take. In general, pacifists joined with isolationists in calling for strict, mandatory neutrality, while internationalists favored some degree of presidential discretion.

During the 1930s the peace movement found a base of public support that was larger than ever before. It has been estimated that during the course of the decade the peace movement reached between 40 and 65 million Americans. Like the peace societies themselves, the groups for which peace had the greatest appeal were many and varied, but the greatest support for the peace makers can be placed in three categories: women, church groups, and students. Throughout the decade, church groups became increasingly concerned with preventing a second world war, and they were especially attracted by the religious and moral convictions of the pacifists. Historically peace-oriented churches, including the Mennonites, Quakers, and Brethren, had the largest pacifist-inclined memberships but failed, on the whole, to play a leading role in the overall movement toward peace. Support from Protestant churches, though smaller in number, was disproportionately vocal. The Protestant clergy, in particular, ardently embraced the cause of peace. Although the laity did not respond to the appeal of peace as heartily, and pacifists remained a minority in Protestant churches, peace-oriented Protestants were extremely successful in shaping the policies of the churches toward their cause. Jewish religious opinion also supported the peace effort, as did, to a lesser extent, Catholic opinion.

The appeal of peace was perhaps felt most strongly by women. A number of the most active peace societies were women's organizations. The Women's International League for Peace and Freedom, for example, was especially active in mobilizing public opinion in support of neutrality legislation. The visibility of female support for the peace movement had a significant effect upon political leaders who feared that women's organizations for peace would have an undue influence upon female voters as a bloc.

The last major group to which the peace movement appealed was made up of college students. Beginning in 1934, nationwide strikes against war were held on college campuses, drawing large numbers of supporters. It is estimated that some 60,000 students participated in such a strike in 1935. The radical wing of the peace movement was particularly active in organizing students against war. The American League Against War and Facism, for example, maintained close ties with two student peace organizations, the American Student Union and the American Youth Congress, urging students toward militant protest against war.

Pacifists, isolationists, and Republicans supported legislation for peace. Two months before the Italian invasion, Congress had passed the First Neutrality Act. Under this measure, the president, at his discretion, could proclaim that a state of war existed; in that event, an embargo on arms, munitions, and implements of war would go into effect. Americans could travel on belligerent-owned ships at their own risk. The measure had several weaknesses: first, it left the decision on the existence of a state of war to the president rather than making it automatic; second, the bill made no distinction between an aggressor and his victim, and this meant that the United States might want to help a defenseless nation but could not; third, it did not define the implements of war but left that up to the president. The last feature enabled the Americans to sell Italy oil and other materials even though Roosevelt had proclaimed the provisions of the act in effect.

In February 1936, Congress passed the Second Neutrality Act. This extended the original provisions fourteen months and, in addition, prohibited loans to the belligerent powers. It required the president to extend the arms embargo to any third power; for example, if Britain had come to the support of Ethiopia, the United States would then have to apply the arms embargo to Britain.

But no sooner had the Middle Eastern crisis ended with the Italian conquest of Ethiopia than a new crisis broke out in Spain. In July 1936 General Francisco Franco and his army supporters revolted against the Spanish government, and for the next three years a bitter civil war took place with Franco supported by Hitler and Mussolini and the Spanish government supported by the Soviet Union. Both the Fascists and the Communists poured supplies and volunteers into the Spanish civil war; its battles became the testing ground for much of the equipment used during the early days of the Second World War.

Unsure of what to do since the existing temporary neutrality legislation did not include provisions for civil wars, the Roosevelt administration hesitated. Congress finally extended the Second Neutrality Act provisions to cover the civil war. In that same year (April 1937) it also passed the third, or permanent, Neutrality Act. This legislation extended indefinitely both the arms embargo and the prohibition against loans. Americans were no longer just warned against traveling on belligerent ships but expressly forbidden to do so. An important new "cash-and-carry" provision prohibited American ships from carrying nonembargoed shipments, and belligerent cargo ships could not leave American shores until payment was made for the cargo in advance. This particular proposal, never put into effect under this act, lasted only until May 1939.

The purpose of the neutrality acts, to guarantee peace for Americans by legislation, had wide support. The acts sought to prevent a repetition of the practices held responsible for bringing the United States into the First World War; indeed, as some writers have pointed out, they tried to prevent American entrance into the First World War some twenty years too late. The greatest weakness of the acts, the failure to make distinctions between aggressors and victims, bothered many Americans. But the acts reflected a sincere belief on the part of a majority of Americans that unilateral legislative actions could maintain peace and keep the United States out of war. After all, who really cared what happened in Manchuria, much less Ethiopia?

Another example of the strong isolationist trend, the proposal by Democratic Representative Louis Ludlow of Indiana for a constitutional amendment requiring a war referendum, also had strong support. Beginning in 1934, Ludlow presented his amendment each year, but not until 1938 did Congress actually vote on it. This amendment said that "except in the event of an invasion of the United States or its territorial possessions and attack upon it citizens . . . the authority of congress to declare war shall not become effective until confirmed by a majority of all votes cast therein in a nation-wide referendum." President Roosevelt and Secretary Hull spoke strongly against the amendment and let their positions become known. While the amendment never passed Congress, the very existence of the issue testified to the strong doubts about the wisdom of having entered the First World War.

During Roosevelt's first term of office, foreign affairs definitely took a back seat to domestic politics. His theory, that the United States must solve its own economic problems before moving on to any foreign ones, had a flaw in that the first phase of the New Deal did not bring the expected recovery or prosperity, although Roosevelt's bold policies did relieve some of the suffering of the depression. And a narrow national interest that seemed to exclude the revival of world trade hurt everyone. Led by the United States, a vicious cycle of tariff restrictions by all countries had ensued; economic nationalism crippled all nations. By 1937, economically or politically, America could no longer afford to duck its head in a hole and ignore the rest of the world. Roosevelt's first public step toward internationalism, the famous quarantine speech of October 1937, in Chicago, tested public opinion. In it he described a "reign of terror and international lawlessness" of epidemic proportions. His solution—"When an epidemic of physical disease starts to spread, the community approves and joins in a quarantine of the patients in order to protect the health of the community against the spread of the disease." The nations of the world led by the United States should band together since "America hates war, America hopes for peace. Therefore America actively engages in the search of peace." These ideas, presented much too suddenly, much too spontaneously, led to a furor. Attacked

Cartoon: "A Good Time for Reflection," 1938.

from all sides, by the isolationists for going too far and by the internationalists for not going far enough, Roosevelt found little support. One of the few setbacks of his political career, criticism of his proposal may well account for his reluctance openly to commit himself in the years to come. From this time on, Roosevelt, in one of the great mistakes of his administration, overestimated the strength of the isolationists. Public sentiment often led the president, rather than the president leading public sentiment. Prime Minister Neville Chamberlain sadly said, "It is always best and safest to count on nothing from the Americans but words."

Public opinion has always played a role in democratic societies, but until the popularization of democracy it was not measurable between elections. The faulty efforts to predict the election outcome in 1936 by the *Literary Digest* constituted one of the early, unsuccessful efforts to assess opinion on political and social issues. Other pioneers were more successful. *Fortune* Magazine began its survey conducted by Elmo Roper in July 10, 1935, and heralded it as a "New Technique in Journalism." Roper and the poll had remarkably good success in forecasting the presidential elections of 1936, 1940, and 1944. George Gallup conducted a series of surveys which were reported in newspapers and widely read and quoted. The *Fortune* Survey noted in mid-1939 that it had found out a lot about public opinion and "one of the significant findings was that public opinion changes, but slowly." *Fortune*'s polls demonstrated that public opinion did change slowly, but when hostilities occurred, as the survey later noted, "public opinion might change very rapidly indeed."

As the German and Japanese adventurism increased, the *Fortune* poll turned its attention toward issues of foreign policy. In the survey of July 1938, 54.8 percent of the respondents approved of the policies of the president. Of the "national population" as *Fortune* identified it, 61.6 percent approved of his international policy, and 69.8 percent approved of his rearmament policy. A year later in the last poll before war began in Europe, the question was asked, "If France and England went to war against the dictator, should the United States send its army to assist them?" While 24.5 percent indicated "only if they were losing," 65.6 percent of the respondents declared, "Not under any circumstances." The *Fortune* Survey astutely observed as a result of those findings that "we may preach peace so long as we risk nothing for it." The same poll, however, asked, "If the Japanese were to seize the Philippines should we get out and stay out?" In this case 50.1 percent replied "no," and only 24.1 percent said "yes" to giving up American control of the Philippines.

Immediately after the war was declared in Europe the President's popularity surged dramatically. From mid-August 1939 to mid-September 1939 favorable response to his international policy increased from 48.5 percent to 69.2 percent. An additional 11.7 percent declared that they partly approved of the president's policy, thus giving him an astounding 80.9 percent approval rate. A month later, however, the same question measured an approval rate of only 56.2 percent. The ebb tide of war in Europe, over which the president had no influence, had much to do with Americans' opinion about his policies.

Meanwhile, other efforts were underway in an attempt to utilize the new process for measuring public attitudes. George Gallup's American Institute of Public Opinion at Princeton institutionalized the process of polling and disseminating results. In 1940, Hadley Cantril, also at Princeton, established the Office of Public Opinion Research with a Rockefeller Foundation grant. Soon thereafter, a confidant of the president, Anna Rosenberg, informed Cantril that Mr. Roosevelt had an interest in his survey work and wanted a specific question to be periodically repeated in the polling. In July 1940 that question regarding American aid to England even at the risk of war, resulted in 37 percent being supportive and 59 percent rejecting aid. By February 1941, the public mood had changed, and the poll showed that 65 percent of respondents expressed approval of the concept of lend-lease. Cantril's liberal philosophy made him useful and trustworthy to the White House, while Gallup, because of his Republican ties, was not so esteemed.

In a relatively short time a measuring tool for political opinion had been honed to a fine edge. During the crucial period from 1939 to 1941 the president demonstrated considerable interest in findings that would reveal how far and how fast he had moved the American public toward an acceptance of actions and policies he believed to be inevitable. The best insight into public opinion came from one of the earlier observers and analysts of it, Walter Lippmann. As he surveyed the role of public opinion in American democracy, Lippmann noted that issues, particularly of foreign affairs, were too complex and too remote for more than a handful of American citizens to be qualified to offer valid opinions. He suggested the role of public opinion in a democracy is of importance only in time of crisis. In his classic *The Public Philosophy*, Lippmann observed that experience teaches us "that in matters of war and peace the popular answer in the democracies is likely to be No." Dexter Perkins did not agree with Lippmann's assessment of public opinion in the prewar years and argued that mass opinion was favorable to preparing for war while we were still at peace, "not so early as might have been wished but as soon as the peril became a lively one."

Richard W. Steele analyzed the Roosevelt administration's use of the media and concluded that an effective public relations program was "a necessary part of government." President Roosevelt's staff realized that the validity of their case would not automatically ensure the public's acceptance of it. Or to contradict Justice Holmes, truth does not always out. Consequently, for the Roosevelt administration, access to the mass media was as important as was the story to be told. Fireside chats, personal talks with media and movie personalities, and an apparent sensitivity to the work of pollsters all mark the Roosevelt years. Steele suggest that the "President-as-propagandist" was a major aspect of Roosevelt's success. President Roosevelt and most of his successors learned that democratic society is by nature passive. The effective use of mass media can transform public opinion at least to an acceptance of new policies in foreign and domestic affairs. As Steele observed of FDR, "his channels to the public mind were deliberately constructed and carefully maintained."

As the fateful day that was to change the course of history drew nearer at the end of 1941, it was preceded by an increasingly expert and effective campaign on the part of the White House to secure public acceptance for policies that in and of themselves could never be popular. When the difficult decisions between 1938 and 1941 were being made, public opinion was being drawn irrevocably to a point where complete and total commitment to a two-front war against two incredibly powerful adversaries was a forgone conclusion on the morning of December 7, 1941.

Selected Reading

The most useful description of Roosevelt's foreign policy is in Robert Dallek's *Franklin D. Roosevelt and American Foreign Policy, 1932–1945* (1979). James MacGregor Burns's *Roosevelt: The Lion and the Fox* (1960) is readable and important. Neither Frank Freidel's *Roosevelt*, 4 vols. (1952–1973), nor Arthur M. Schlesinger, Jr.'s *The Age of Roosevelt*, 3 vols. (1957–1960), has managed to get beyond the 1930s in their classic but unfinished biographies; both include favorable interpretations of Roosevelt's conduct of foreign policy. *Franklin D. Roosevelt and the New Deal, 1932–1940* (1963) by William E. Leuthtenburg provides a good brief overview of the domestic imperatives of FDR. Robert Divine's *The Reluctant Belligerent* (1965) is a good introduction to the 1930s foreign policy. For a valuable treatment of public opinion in this period, see Richard W. Steele's *Propaganda in an Open Society: The Roosevelt Administration and the Media, 1933–1941* (1985).

Secretary of State Cordell Hull's *Memoirs*, 2 vols. (1948), are dull but rewarding. Richard N. Current is critical in *Secretary Stimson: A Study in Statecraft* (1954). The view from the secretary of the treasury can be found in John Morton Blum's *From the Morgenthau Diaries*, Vol. 1: *Years of Crisis, 1928–1938* (1959). Fred L. Israel's *Nevada's Key Pittman* (1963) on the chairman of the Senate Foreign Relations Committee is revealing.

On relations with Russia, Joan Hoff Wilson's *Ideology and Economics: U.S. Relations with the Soviet Union, 1918–1933* (1974) is an important work, as is Edward M. Bennett's *Recognition of Russia: An American Foreign Policy Dilemma* (1970). Two works by George Kennan, *Russia and the West Under Lenin and Stalin* (1960) and volume one of his *Memoirs: 1925–1950* (1967) present a realist perspective. *William C. Bullitt and The Soviet Union* (1967) by Beatrice Farnsworth discusses the intriguing first American ambassador to the Soviet Union.

Arnold A. Offner's fine *American Appeasement: United States Foreign Policy and Germany, 1933–1938* (1969) is critical of American policy. *Mussolini and Fascism: The View from America* (1972) by John Diggins surveys American opinion. Christopher Thorne's definitive *The Limits of Foreign Policy: The West, the League and the Far Eastern Crisis of 1931–1933* (1972) and Dorothy Borg's *The United States and the Far Eastern Crisis of 1933–1938* (1964) are solid works on the Manchurian crisis. Also useful are the excellent essays on statesmen in Richard Dean Burns and Edward M. Bennett, eds., *Diplomats in Crisis: United States-Chinese-Japanese Relations 1919–1941* (1974).

The military/strategy issues are treated in Raymond G. O'Connor, *Perilous Equilibrium: The United States and the London Conference of 1930* (1962) and Lester H. Brune, *The Origins of American National Security Policy: Sea Power, Air Power, and Foreign Policy, 1900–1941* (1981). Two works that cover European military events are useful for comparative purposes: Brian Bond's *British Military Policy Between the Two World Wars* (1980) and Barry R. Posen's *The Sources of Military Doctrine* (1984). Two interesting studies that in part touch this period are Russell F. Weigley, *The American Way of War: A History of United States Military Strategy and Policy* (1973) and Samuel P. Huntington, *The Soldier and the State: The Theory and Politics of Civil Military Relations* (1957).

Information on peace movements can best be found in Charles Chatfield, *For Peace and Justice* (1971), Charles DeBenedetti, *The Peace Reform in American History* (1980), and Solomon Wank, ed., *Doves and Diplomats: Foreign Offices and Peace Movements in Europe and America in the Twentieth Century* (1978). John Edward Wiltz's *In Search of Peace: The Senate Munitions Inquiry, 1934–1936* (1963) is excellent.

Michael Leigh in his *Mobilizing Consent, Public Opinion and American Foreign Policy, 1937–1947* (1976) deals with Roosevelt's relations with the press and public relations.

7 Roads to War

The United States followed two roads in traveling to the Second World War: one European, the other East Asian. While for purposes of narrative we will travel both of these roads separately, it is important to remember that they often criss-crossed and followed each other. The surprise came when the United States reached its destination at the end of the East Asian journey first. For the European road had the familiar episodes of sinking ships and submarines, much like the First World War, with the possibility of going to war clearly in sight well before the end of the trip. The East Asian road, however, was longer, winding, unpaved, filled with diplomatic chuckholes, and unplanned detours and led to a destination of war that was as unexpected as was its form of an ambush at Pearl Harbor. To question the necessity of even taking the Japanese trip, prior to the completion of the more important German one, suggests a possible alternative to what actually happened. And at least one scholar contends that the American government should have taken neither road and remained entirely out of the Second World War since the results, in his opinion, were so unwelcome. Whatever the strength of these suggestions, and we shall return to these questions, what the United States did along the way to the Second World War had considerable impact on both the fighting and results of the war.

In January 1938, Roosevelt asked Congress for a billion dollar naval appropriation, which Congress promptly gave him; but by this time neither the quarantine speech nor American rearmament plans could stop Hitler and Nazi Germany. Hitler announced the annexation of **139**

Austria to Germany in March; he then turned to the neighboring state of Czechoslovakia. The British Prime Minister, Neville Chamberlain, tried to prevent the German advance by proposing a conference. Hitler, delighted, privately said he would talk to the British "schweinhund." After this first summit conference, Chamberlain came away saying that he had the "impression that Hitler was a man who could be relied upon when he had given his word" and Hitler had sworn he would not march. On September 30, representatives of Germany, Italy, France, and Britain met in Munich to discuss the situation. The resultant agreement turned over the Czech Sudetenland to Germany; in Hitler's words, the "last territorial claim I shall make in Europe." Chamberlain, umbrella in hand, proclaimed the Munich agreement "peace in our time." In March 1939 the Germans gobbled up all of Czechoslovakia, thereby breaking the Munich agreement, and in the process capturing tons of modern war materials that made future aggression much easier. Which way next? In August of 1939 the answer came when, to the amazement of the world, the Soviets and Germans signed a nonaggression pact. By its secret protocol the Nazis laid claim to western Poland and the Russians claimed the Baltic states and eastern Poland. The treaty was followed with the September 1939 invasion of Poland by Germany. The Second World War officially started as England and France declared war on Germany.

The initial aggressions of Nazi Germany met nothing but useless words in return from America. Roosevelt tried to use his prestige by appealing to the "peaceful" instincts of Hitler and Mussolini. Shortly before the Munich conference, the president had sent a personal appeal to the two men, but with little result. Roosevelt attempted the same thing in April of 1939 when he asked Hitler and Mussolini to promise not to attack some thirty-one countries in the Middle East and Europe. Hitler commented on his willingness to sign nonaggression pacts with any country, but none had asked. Roosevelt began to realize that his words, unsupported by military force, had no influence on the European aggressors. After the beginning of the war in September 1939, Roosevelt officially proclaimed American neutrality, but he said he would not ask, as Wilson had, that "Americans remain neutral in thought as well as in deed." FDR said "even a neutral cannot be asked to close his mind or his conscience." With the proclamation of neutrality, the arms embargo went into effect.

Roosevelt then tried to bring about a revision of the arms embargo and other neutrality legislation. With the passage of the Neutrality Act of 1939 (or Fourth Neutrality Act) all belligerents could purchase arms, ammunition, and implements of war, but only on a cash-and-carry basis. The act prohibited loans and forbade the entrance of American ships and travelers into combat zones designated by the president. This bill, the result of a compromise between the administration and the isolationists, did let FDR send arms and munitions to Britain and France.

Roosevelt, privately, had made up his mind to support the Allies to the limit of America's capacity, but he did not tip his hand until almost the end of 1940; and he tried to deal only with each situation as it came up. His caution continued to reflect his healthy respect for the isolationist forces in the public and in Congress. Public discussion over neutrality and the extent to which the United States should support the Allies became intensive in 1940. The America First Committee gave leadership to the isolationists. Headed by such prominent figures as Charles A. Lindbergh, Robert E. Wood, Henry Ford, and Chester Bowles, this group did not want to enter the war, but preferred to keep the United States independent of the European struggle. The Committee to Defend America by Aiding the Allies, headed by William A. White, was the most important opposing pressure group; White, in close touch with FDR, succeeded in arousing a large segment of public opinion to support his policies.

In April 1940, the Germans struck at Norway and Denmark, and in May the Germans marched into France. Only the miracle at Dunkirk succeeded in saving any part of the British and French armies. The Italians joined in the attack, and on June 22 the French had to accept Hitler's armistice terms at Compiègne in the very railroad car in which the Germans had surrendered to the French in 1918. The reaction in America came quickly. Roosevelt asked Congress to increase America's armed forces and to step up the production of war materials; he also, at Charlottesville, Virginia, on June 11, promised aid to those nations opposing aggressors. Roosevelt attempted to gain bipartisan support for his program by appointing two Republicans to his cabinet, Henry Stimson as secretary of war and Frank Knox as secretary of the navy. Both men advocated aid to the Allies. In the Act of Havana of July 30, 1940, representatives of the nations of the Western Hemisphere pledged that they would resist European aggressors who attempted to take over the colonies of their victims in the Western Hemisphere. The Roosevelt administration also began to make joint plans for defense with the Canadian government.

The American army remained strongly isolationist in outlook, opposed to overseas commitments that it did not have the military power to defend, and deeply suspicious of attempts by the British to entangle the United States once again in European difficulties, as they had so cleverly done in 1917. But even if isolationist, the army took a very broad view, including the entire hemisphere within its defense perimeter. David G. Haglund, in a most insightful work, makes a convincing case that for the American military "the defense of the United States also entailed the defense of much of Latin America. . . . The most vital national interest, the physical security of the United States was deemed to be contingent upon the maintenance of a Western hemisphere immune to the contagion of a European war." Europe remained to many army officers an undesirable environment that American military forces should stay out of; there was nothing in Europe worth fighting for. The Germans and the Italians, however, were making inroads in Latin America; by 1936, for example, Germany had replaced Great Britain as the largest exporter of goods to Latin America (the United States was first) and there were large settlements of Germans and Italians in Brazil and Argentina. Haglund concludes that it was the perception of that threat to this hemisphere, and no particular support for Great Britain, that led first the military and then the president to connect the preservation of Great Britain in 1940, thereby tying up German-Italian ambitions, with the maintenance of security for the Western Hemisphere. Even with the coming of war in 1941, nevertheless, the army retained its Anglophobic, isolationist outlook.

Lieutenant General Stanley Embick was representative of army officers who had developed hemispheric viewpoints. He, and many others, felt that the Philippines were a strategic liability that might provoke the Japanese to mount an attack that the army would have little or no chance of withstanding. Embick was to oppose FDR's plans for armed escorts in the Atlantic in 1941 since they would involve the danger of provoking the Germans and would take vital military supplies away from the defense of the hemisphere.

In 1940 a major escalation occured in the destroyers-for-bases deal with Great Britain. Churchill, who had become prime minister in 1940, asked Roosevelt for the loan of forty to fifty old American destroyers to combat the increasingly effective German submarines. Roosevelt knew the importance of immediate aid for the British, but he faced a legal problem. To turn over such material he had to certify the equipment as nonessential for the national defense of the United States, and his military leaders, General George C. Marshall and Admiral Harold E. Stark, proved unwilling to make such a certification. After some hesitation, for FDR feared that congress would flatly turn down such a proposal, his advisers came up with another idea. Why not exchange the destroyers for the release of British naval bases in the Western Hemisphere, such as those in Newfoundland and Bermuda? This, of course, would add to the defense of the Americas. Churchill later described the consumation of the arrangement as "a decidely unneutral act by the United States," that would have justified a German declaration of war. It ended any pretense of American neutrality.

Right in the middle of all the debate over foreign policy came the presidential election of 1940, which surely must rank as one of the most distorted elections in American political history. The Republican platform favored aid "not in violation of international law" and firmly opposed "involving this nation in foreign war"; the Democratic platform pledged aid but also said: "We will not participate in foreign war, and we will not send our army, naval or air forces to fight in foreign lands outside of the Americas, except in case of attack." The Republicans, in one of the great surprises of political history, nominated an unknown Indiana lawyer, Wendell L. Willkie, and the Democrats, informed at the last moment that FDR wanted a third term, duly renominated the president.

Willkie at a disadvantage in that he agreed with the general objectives of the president's program did deliver some telling blows on the methods, errors, and shortcomings of the administration's policies. At this point

Europe, 1936–1939

he quarreled more with the president's methods than with his goals. Roosevelt kept quiet until October when Willkie began to state that he would never lead America into a war. In one speech Willkie said that "If the [president's] promise to keep our boys out of foreign wars is no better than his promise to balance the budget, they're already almost on the transports." The president's political advisers told him that if he wanted to win he had better speak out for peace. FDR proceeded to do so by saying that "It is for peace that I have labored; and it is for peace that I shall labor all the days of my life." But Roosevelt's sincere statements about peace straddled the essence of the issue. Willkie's charges revolved around the accusation that the methods the president used to carry out his foreign policy, and particularly the program of aid to Britain by all means short of war, involved the clear risk of ultimate American involvement in the hostilities. On this crucial issue, Roosevelt had nothing to say to the American people during the campaign. On October 30, 1940, in Baltimore, Willkie said, sensing an important issue, "you may expect we will be at war," if the president won.

That same night Roosevelt spoke in Boston. He had decided to announce a program to permit the British to place orders for billions of dollars worth of new munitions as a positive commitment to the British. But Roosevelt's advisers continued to ask him also to say something about peace, and F.D.R. responded. The words may have seemed meaningless to him, but they echoed sufficiently clear to the American people. He said, "And while I am talking to you mothers and fathers I give you one more assurance. I have said this before, but I shall say it again and again: Your boys are not going to be sent into any foreign wars. . . . The purpose of defense is defense." Nothing that Roosevelt said in the 1940 campaign is so remembered as this statement in Boston. Whether Roosevelt's positive stance led to Willkie's defeat is unknown; most historians believe that Roosevelt would have won under any circumstances. But the president seriously weakened the cause he sought to advance and certainly added no luster to his reputation for sincerity and openness. After Pearl Harbor he said that no war Americans fought in deserved the title of a "foreign war."

After the smoke of the election had cleared, the victorious Roosevelt, perhaps in part because of his election pledges, moved very slowly.

Churchill wrote that he no longer feared the possibility of an invasion by Germany, but the German submarine campaign had Great Britain in serious difficulty. The prime minister wanted the Americans to carry goods in their own ships and to transfer more destroyers, as well as cargo ships, to Britain. More important, he also warned that the British had all but exhausted their cash reserves and would soon need loans. Roosevelt's Secretary of Navy Frank Knox and Secretary of War Henry Stimson expressed absolute certainty that the Roosevelt administration would sooner or later have to aid Britain militarily. The president said that he wanted to get away from the dollar sign, that he did not want to give aid to the Allies with an emphasis on dollars or loans. Obviously the president did not want a repetition of the war debt problem of the First World War.

In a press conference the trend of Roosevelt's thought became clarified. He said, "Suppose my neighbor's home catches fire, and I have a length of garden hose. . . . Now what do I do? I don't say to him . . . Neighbor, my garden hose cost me $15; you have to pay me $15 for it—I want my garden hose back after the fire is over." In a speech later that month, Roosevelt argued that an Axis victory would pose a great threat to the United States. Because of that threat the American nation must send Britain all the supplies it needed in order to withstand the Nazis. FDR said, "We must become the great arsenal of democracy." He believed that supplying the Allies with war materials involved the least risk for the United States and the greatest chance for peace in the future.

In January 1941 the president presented his plan of aid to Congress. He felt that the United States could not tell nations defending themselves against Axis attack to surrender merely because they had exhausted their cash supply. Instead the American government should supply them and postpone a decision about the form of repayment until the future. He concluded that he looked forward to "a world founded upon four essential freedoms—freedom of speech and expression, freedom of religion, freedom from want, and freedom from fear."

A few days later, the Roosevelt administration introduced a bill "to promote the Defense of the United States," numbered House Resolution 1776, better known as Lend-Lease. This bill would grant the president broad powers to sell, lease, or lend defense articles to the government of any country whose defense the president thought vital to the defense of the United States. In return for such help, repayment would take place in any manner determined acceptable by the president. In substance, Roosevelt wanted from Congress a blank check that he would fill in.

Opposition to the bill immediately developed among the traditionalists and isolationists. Senator Burton K. Wheeler, Democratic senator from Montana, led off with a blast against FDR. "Never before," he said, "has the United States given to one man the power to strip this Nation of its defenses. Never before has a congress coldly and flatly been asked to abdicate. . . . The Lend Lease-give program is the New Deal's triple-A foreign policy: it will plow under every fourth American boy." Roosevelt, deeply angered, replied that Wheeler's statement represented the most "dastardly, unpatriotic thing that has ever been said. That really is the rottenest thing that has been said in public life in my generation."

The great argument went on. In general the administration's supporters presented the bill as primarily designed to protect the nation's security without bringing about military intervention. They did not believe that Hitler would use the bill as an excuse to declare war on the United States; they did believe the bill would prevent a shooting war. Opponents of Lend-Lease centered their attack on the concentration of power the bill would give the president, and they tried to present all the future implications of the act. Opponents argued that sooner or later, and probably sooner, the American government would have to convoy the goods to the Allies and enter the war itself if the Germans attempted to prevent the shipments. The Roosevelt administration stated that the bill would keep the United States out of the war. In retrospect, the isolationists, correct in their contention that passage of Lend-Lease would lead to certain logical steps down the road to war, had a good argument and some colorful speakers; they did not, however, have the votes. The president had the numbers, and for this reason in March 1941 the Lend-Lease bill passed Congress (final votes—60-31 in the Senate and 317-71 in the House), and Congress appropriated $7 billion to carry out the program. The importance of Lend-Lease cannot be overstated. Lend-Lease not only made possible an enormous initial expansion of American war industries, paid for by the British orders, but, more important, the act represented an American commitment to support the Allies to the greatest extent of its resources. Hitler certainly could have declared war on legitimate grounds, the only question after the passage of Lend-Lease was not whether war with Germany would come, but when.

At this point two important events occured with respect to the Axis powers. In 1940 Japan, Italy, and Germany signed the Tripartite Pact, in which the Germans recognized Japanese leadership in East Asia and in return received economic privileges from Japan. The pact, clearly a warning to the United States, since the arrangement specifically exempted the Soviet Union, also provided for military cooperation if any of the three powers found themselves under attack by a nation not already in war. Hitler wanted at this time, and later, the Japanese to attack the Soviet Union in Siberia. The Japanese refused Hitler's request and saved the Soviet Union from a double invasion that might well have destroyed the Russian regime. In April of 1941, the Japanese signed a nonaggression pact with the Soviet Union in which each power pledged to remain neutral for five years if the other should become involved in war. In June Nazi Germany, in its most fateful gamble, invaded the Soviet Union.

This raised the problem in the democracies of whether to aid the communists. Churchill, an old Bolshevik hater, had no hesitation and said, "I have only one purpose, the destruction of Hitler, and my life is much simplified hereby. If Hitler invaded Hell, I would make at least a favorable reference to the Devil in the House of Commons." The British position made it easier for the president to make up his mind to aid the Russians. Some Americans, among them Senator Harry S Truman of Missouri, suggested that Americans should let the Germans and Russians kill each other; still others placed Communist Russia as a far more dangerous threat to the peace of the world than Nazi Germany.

In August of 1941, unknown to most of the world, President Roosevelt and Prime Minister Churchill met at sea, off the coast of Newfoundland. This meeting marked the culmination of more than a year of close diplomatic relations between the two, established a pattern of coalition summit conference, and brought forth the Atlantic Charter. The two leaders first talked about how they could speed up aid to the Allies, including Russia. Churchill also wanted to send a joint ultimatum to the Japanese, but Roosevelt refused. The Atlantic Charter, however, provided the most memorable point of the conference. Roosevelt did not want a repetition of the embarrassing secret treaties, such as had occurred in the First World War, dividing up the world between the Allies if they won. With that bit of history in mind, the two leaders decided to publish a statement of their ideals. This declaration of August 14, 1941, called for no territorial claims; for people to have the right to chose their own form of government; for equality of trade; for a peace that would afford safety to all men that they might live out their lives in freedom from fear and want; for freedom of the seas; and for disarmament. The charter, often compared to Wilson's Fourteen Points, was an unusual statement of war aims. Almost meaninglessly vague, ambiguous, and even contradictory, so carefully worded it represents no more than a publicity handout, it was in actual form a joint press release. As a basis for postwar peace, people of the world could read into it whatever they pleased. Considering the Atlantic Charter outlined a declaration of war aims, unusual to say the least for a neutral such as the United States, vagueness perhaps had a definite place in its formulation and presentation.

With the Atlantic Conference and passage of Lend-Lease the survival of Great Britain had become the major goal of American policy. Yet realistic observers knew the necessity of still stronger measures if that goal also envisioned the defeat of the Axis Powers. In September 1941 the heads of the army and navy informed FDR that if Germany was to be militarily defeated, the armed forces of the United States would have to take part in the war. Roosevelt still hesitated, in part because of his previous statements, to take the final step of actually asking for a war declaration. Consequently, the president edged along, leaving it up to Hitler to make the choice of measures that might bring about an all-out war. FDR could actually push quite far at this time without bringing about a retaliation from Hitler, since the Germans, tied up in Russia, did not want to divert crucial forces to fight the Americans. Soon, however, escorts of American naval ships, whether in patrol or convoy,

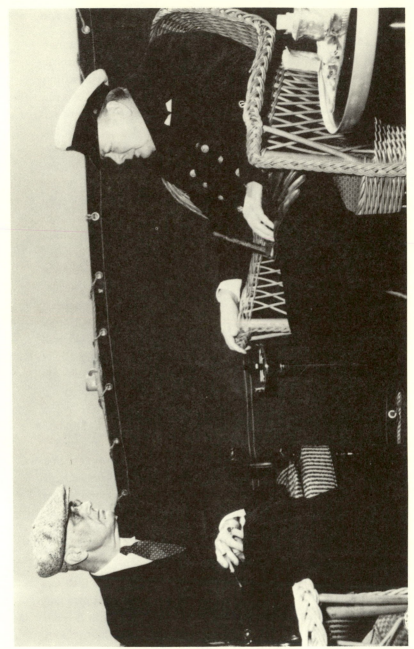

Roosevelt and Churchill at Yalta.

traveled with British ships long distances in the Atlantic and sometimes as far as Iceland and Greenland. Sooner or later trouble would develop as Americans tried to protect their Lend-Lease supplies to Great Britain.

On September 4, 1941, an American destroyer, the *USS Greer*, in route to Iceland, cooperated with a British plane in locating and trailing a German submarine. After several hours the submarine sent a warning torpedo across the bow of the destroyer, and the *Greer* fought back by dropping depth charges. FDR in a fireside chat on September 11 ingeniously said the submarine had fired first with the deliberate intention of sinking the *Greer*. He then announced shoot-on-sight orders to the United States Navy. In an attempt to place the responsibility on the Germans, Roosevelt presented the circumstances of the *Greer* attack in a less than candid manner by obscuring the extent of its cooperation with the British. A loss of eleven American lives on the destroyer *USS Kearny* occurred on October 17. Again FDR went to the airways and said "America has been attacked. The USS *Kearny* is not just a Navy ship. She belongs to every man, woman, and child in this Nation." Roosevelt neglected to say that the *Kearny*, when torpedoed, was attacking German submarines. Other incidents followed in the fall of 1941 (for example, *Reuben James*, October 30, with a loss of 96 lives). By a series of strong acts, the United States government had aligned itself with the Allies against Germany; Hitler certainly recognized the United States as his enemy. In the winter of 1941–1942 war with Germany loomed.

Roosevelt's deviousness with the American people raises serious questions about the conduct of foreign policy in a democracy. Certainly his acts were those of an imperial presidency unconcerned with the niceties of the Constitution. Greater openness might well have provoked a domestic debate, as he feared, but if the goal were indeed desirable, such a debate would have been more in keeping with democratic traditions and might well have won support. FDR's desire for a certain goal again led him to ignore the correctness of the means necessary to attain the end result. The essence of democracy is surely a concern with means as well as ends.

The Japanese, as noted previously, had taken their first step along the road to aggression with the invasion of Manchuria in 1931. Here in the northernmost provinces of China, the Japanese, in defiance of the League of Nations, had carved out the puppet state of Manchukuo, which then became a springboard to the interior of China itself. A peace of sorts transpired between the Chinese and Japanese from 1934 until 1937; in the latter year, an all-out, but undeclared, war broke out.

The United States Navy Board viewed the events of 1931 and 1932 with concern, as did the rest of the world. Japan had set upon the course of creating an empire in Asia. The Navy Board noted that the Philippine Islands stood in the way of further expansion by Japan toward Southeast Asia. The Navy Board informed the Joint Board that it was unable, under current force limitations and budgetary restraints, to defend the Philippines from the Japanese if that contingency became necessary. Whatever the Joint Board and President Hoover and later President Roosevelt may have believed, the Navy Board continued to assume that the United States would eventually be at war with Japan.

American diplomats were less concerned about the military events in Asia. The State Department followed the lead of President Roosevelt and assumed that the long-term interests of the United States lay with events in Europe more than with those in Asia. Both Germany and Italy provided good cause for that concern. The American armed forces, however, and specifically the Joint Board saw the primary military problem as being the defense of American territory which was clearly at risk in Asia and in the Pacific. To the military, American territory was to be defended, however difficult the task or remote the territory. The State Department viewed historical American interests as linked to those of Europe. The wars and alliances that had most affected the United States had emanated from European capitals and the close ties to Great Britain and France that were created in the First World War placed Europe at the center of the United States' planning for future American security. This Janus-like stance put the United States in the posture of having its military looking to the Pacific and its diplomacy looking to the Atlantic for future security. In the early years of both a maturing military establishment and diplomatic corps, there was fundamental disagreement about threats and priorities. A national security policy languished in such an environment.

The Axis Powers simplified the dichotomous posture of the United

States by signing an Anti-Comintern Pact in the Winter of 1936–1937. The act assisted President Roosevelt in making a decision he had thus far avoided. He asked the Joint Board to provide an update of its war plans. That request, which came in January 1937, stimulated the navy to reaffirm its Orange Plan and call for the building of its long awaited Pacific fleet. As the navy was sadly to learn, Roosevelt believed, and never abandoned that belief, that the main American interests were in Europe. There his efforts and attention were to focus.

On July 7, 1937, a skirmish at the Marco Polo Bridge near Peking spawned fighting throughout northern China. The Chinese, even with cooperation between Chiang Kai-shek and the Communists, were unable to stop the Japanese, and by December 1937 the Japanese occupied Nanking. During the surge southward, the Japanese machine-gunned the motorcar of Sir Hugh Knatchbull Hugessen, the British representative to China. He was seriously wounded. The British government protested but followed a course of careful neutrality.

In October 1937 Roosevelt gave his Quarantine Speech, but subsequently he gave no aid to the Chinese nor did he give much solace to the American planners who had hoped to see him embrace the Orange Plan. Instead, the president expressed disapproval of the current war plans with special negative feelings toward the Orange Plan. He informed the Joint Board that he wanted a plan that was based on the defense of the Western Hemisphere and a future two ocean war against Axis Powers with Great Britain as an ally. Publicly, Franklin Roosevelt and his secretary of state, Cordell Hull, repeated the view that world public opinion was a moral force against warfare. As Edward Hallett Carr noted in his study of international relations between the two wars, the American posture of statesmanship was viewed as a sign of "American unwillingness to resort to more potent weapons."

It was some consolation to the navy when the president asked Congress to increase the ship procurement budget for the navy by 20 percent. Congress, the president, and the navy still wanted capital ships for the long-range Pacific fleet while the president, and part of the Congress wanted ships for hemispheric defense.

There were clear signs that the president was altering his stance toward military preparation. While the Joint Board was in a quandary trying to realign its thinking on strategy and war plans, the White House was the scene of increasing meetings between the president, the military, and diplomatic leaders on a variety of matters. The State Department moved to strengthen its link with Great Britain, and Cordell Hull announced the implementation of the Neutrality Act of 1937. Trade flowed steadily to Europe, and the United States chose not to recognize a state of belligerency between China and Japan. By this inaction, the United States could continue to trade with China and hence help her feeble and failing war effort against the Japanese.

Although the infrastructure and bureaucratic organization of a national security policy did not exist in the early years of the Roosevelt Administration, many of the elements of such a policy were there. One of the president's early moves was to begin a reorganization of government in order to provide greater efficiency and faster response to presidential leadership. Initiated in January 1937, the Reorganization Act of 1939 created the Executive Office of the President and placed within it the Bureau of the Budget, the National Resource Planning Board, and the White House Office. The Executive Order that implemented the structure of the Executive Office provided that in the event of a threat of a national emergency, that office would be responsible for management of the emergency as the president determined. Meanwhile the military branches were emerging in the form they would later, by law, take. Air power was developing and asserting influence within command structure. The most notable element of a national security policy also emerged in the second Roosevelt administration—planning.

The Orange Plan had served the planning needs of the Joint Board quite well during most of the interwar period. It was periodically revised but always retained an offensive naval power as the foundation of American security. Franklin Roosevelt was aligned to the navy by past experiences and perhaps by proclivity. In his first year as president he had announced that the navy should construct to treaty strength. A year later Senator Carl Vinson led in the introduction of legislation to use Public Works Administration money to build ships to the limits of the treaty. The navy continued to hold its doctrine of an offensive force during this construction period, although it did give authorization within the building program for the construction of two aircraft carriers. Battle tactics changed as the carrier-based aircraft proved valuable in exercises as an adjunct to the fleet. In 1934 the navy even considered a proposal for a carrier task force. In 1937 the president called for a "two ocean" navy and the new rhetoric quickly replaced the long-held hope for a navy "second-to-none."

As battle exercises changed, tactics were altered, naval aviators became more proficient, and carriers and concomitant aircraft were built, a subtle change occurred in naval capabilities. The navy may not have seemed to notice, but the president did. As part of his efforts to establish national strength in late 1937, the president acknowledged that the navy was to play the primary role, bolstered by coastal defense from the U.S. Army Air Corps.

By the fall of 1938, Roosevelt had pushed the Joint Board toward a new set of war plans. These plans, known as the Rainbow Plans, were based on the fundamentals that the president had imposed upon the military. The war plans assumed that there would be increased friction between the United States, Germany, and Italy. The previously existing plans had already hypothesized potential hostilities with Japan. The new plans also assumed that there would be cooperation among the United States, Great Britain, and France. Further, there would be unity among the nations of the Western Hemisphere. Finally, the plans assumed there would have to be increased diplomatic pressure on Japan in order to avert war in the Pacific. To underscore the Rainbow Plans, the president on October 11, 1938, asked for an increase of $300 million in defense appropriations. A month later he called for the construction of 20,000 airplanes for the military but in January 1939 reduced that figure to a more realistic 6,000.

In response to the president's pressure, the Joint Board approved Rainbow One on August 14, 1939. It called for hemispheric defense as the primary requisite for American defense. Rainbow One had hardly been adopted when war in Europe erupted and caused Rainbow Two to take predominance. It was based upon Great Britain and France defending against the Axis Powers in Europe and the United States defending against Japan in the Pacific. Again the navy had the major role, not greatly different from its own Orange Plan. In this case, however, the plan included the possibility that the United States would

have to defend Singapore, and that did not delight the navy. The fall of France in June 1940 ended the validity of Rainbow Two. It was followed by Rainbow Three and Rainbow Four, which envisioned the United States having to fight Japan with no allies, and, in the case of Rainbow Four, projected a German defeat of Great Britain. President Roosevelt objected to the dire prediction inherent in Rainbow Four, and it never was implemented. Rainbow Five was adopted in May 1941. In it the navy was to fight a defensive war in the Pacific, but the primary units of the fleet would move to the Atlantic where the United States would adopt a Germany-first strategy. This plan also programed the heavy bombing of German positions in Europe as a prelude to an eventual invasion. The army developed a plan called AWPD-1 during the summer of 1941 that would implement the proposed bombing plan. Rainbow Five finally laid Mahan to rest and replaced him with the doctrines of Billy Mitchell. Air power had, on the very eve of American entry into World War II, finally come of age.

Diplomatically, President Roosevelt had reacted to the Sino-Japanese war with the usual protest; but, more importantly, he refused to apply the Neutrality Act to the struggle because of the lack of a declaration of war. This meant that the United States government could continue to help the Chinese. On December 12, 1937, Japanese bombing planes sank a clearly marked American gunboat, the *Panay*, on a Chinese river, along with three American merchant ships. Three Americans died and 74 suffered wounds. The Roosevelt administration sent a stiff note, and the Japanese government, realizing its actions had gone too far, presented an apology and offered to pay an indemnity. But just prior to this incident the Japanese had refused to attend a conference of the signatories of the Nine-Power Treaty of 1922, which had guaranteed the Open Door in China. By now no one expected the Japanese to retreat before a barrage of mere protests. The Japanese pushed ahead in order to finish up the "China incident," as they called it, but Chiang Kai-shek refused to give up.

The Japanese had given some thought to turning north to Siberia after they finished off their work in China, but the Nazi-Soviet pact of 1939 convinced the Japanese that they could not completely trust their Nazi partners. A higher wisdom seemed to indicate a southern turn to the vital raw materials of Southeast Asia, Indochina, Thailand, and the Dutch East Indies, perhaps even the Philippines. The European war presented the Japanese with a golden opportunity to acquire the colonial possessions of France, Great Britain, the Netherlands, and perhaps those of the United States if that nation entered the European war. This fateful decision by the Japanese, when finally implemented in 1941, would directly affect American interests in East Asia.

In 1939 Roosevelt took an action that also proved of the greatest importance in 1941. On July 26, 1939, the president gave the Japanese the required six-months' notice for terminating the Japanese-American commercial treaty of 1911. This meant that after January 1940 the American government could cut off Japanese trade at any moment and, for example, impose embargoes against Japanese purchases. The implied threat behind this action strongly affected the Japanese since they obtained about half of their raw materials from the United States at that time; 80 percent of Japan's scrap iron, steel products, and oil came from America. Neither country wanted hostilities in 1939. The Japanese were not ready for war because they needed to build up their supplies, and to the Roosevelt administration the European stakes loomed larger. Nevertheless, both countries were laying the groundwork for future actions.

The United States government had an additional reason for proceeding cautiously. Within the Japanese government two main groups contended for control of policy. Militarists favored all-out expansion, while the civilian government tried to restrain the militarists not so much by disagreement with their goals, with which they agreed, as by attempting to impede their immediate progress. Timing, more than goals, separated the two. As long as the more peaceful group held a degree of power, the Roosevelt administration did not want to do anything that might upset the balance and bring the militarists to power. The existence of the peaceful group, which was never really strong enough to do more than temporarily hold off the militarists, encouraged the Roosevelt administration to hope for a possible Japanese retreat.

The Japanese continued to negotiate with the United States Department of State. The Japanese asked for recognition of the Co-Prosperity Sphere of Greater East Asia (a sort of Japanese Monroe Doctrine in their eyes), for America's cooperation in inducing Chiang Kai-shek to make peace with the Japanese, for a new trade treaty, for America's help in enabling the Japanese to obtain a fair share of the undeveloped resources of east Asia, and for a loan from the American government. They also wanted the Roosevelt administration to stop any embargoes (such as, for example, a July 31, 1940, embargo on aviation fuel) against Japan. But the Japanese proposals constantly met rejection in Washington. Both Secretary of State Cordell Hull and Roosevelt made it clear that there could be no peaceful settlement unless the Japanese got out of China, respected the Open Door, and abandoned their military adventures. A political agreement could take place only if one or the other side gave in and made substantial concessions. In spite of all the negotiations that took place, the positions of the two countries changed very little from 1937 to 1941. The Japanese tended to talk in terms of specific negotiating bargains, while the Americans replied with general principles. A note by Hull on April 16, 1941, seemed to best summarize the America position. Hull called for four things: 1) "Respect for the territorial integrity and the sovereignty of each and all nations; 2) Support of the principle of non-interference in the internal affairs of other countries; 3) Support of the principle of equality, including equality of commercial opportunity; and 4) Non-disturbance of the status quo in the Pacific except as the status quo may be altered by peaceful means."

At the very base of the trouble between the two nations stood China; the United States refused to abandon China to the Japanese, and the Japanese would not leave. Japan's interests in China were primary, while American interests were secondary. But the United States, especially Cordell Hull, never clearly recognized the importance of that distinction. The American government might best have heeded the wise advice of John Van MacMurray, the former head of the Far Eastern Division of the Department of State. He counseled in 1935 that the United States had three alternatives: 1) to actively oppose Japan; 2) to acquiesce or even participate with the Japanese; or 3) to take a passive attitude. The first would mean war, and "nobody except Russia would gain from our victory in such a war." Indeed the avoidance of a war with Japan would have to be a "major objective" of American policy. Any large opposition to Japanese policies might "lead them to make a

desperate attack" which could "force us into a war we do not want."
MacMurray believed the third alternative was the most feasible: to
maintain American principles "even though we do not find it prudent
to go crusading in furtherance of them." He found no reason for the
United States to make herself a leader of "any forlorn hope for the
purpose of vindicating them in the Far East." The United States had no
mission to undertake any duties or responsibilities in behalf of China,
for China had become an "almost negligible factor," while Japan had
become of "paramount importance." It was time to husband American
strength, to write down American interests in China to their present
"depreciated value," to deal with Japan fairly and sympathetically, to
be guided by the national interest, and not to wander into false trials
whether pro- or anti-Chinese, or pro- or anti-Japanese. MacMurray's
advice was ignored, but it is interesting to note that neither the United
States nor Japan gained in China after the Second World War what it
had asked for in 1941. American policies neither served the cause of
peace nor brought about the triumph of its principles.

It is also of the utmost importance to remember that Great Britain,
with large interests in China, had a crucial influence on American
policies. It is true that Prime Minister Neville Chamberlain, worried
about the American stance in 1937, had said "in the present state of
European affairs with the two dictators in a thoroughly nasty temper
we simply cannot afford to quarrel with Japan and I very much fear
therefore that after a lot of ballyhoo the Americans will somehow fade
out and leave us to carry the blame and odium." Contrary to his fears,
however, the Roosevelt administration saw the connection between Britain's problems in East Asia and the British fight for survival in Europe.
As Great Britan fought in Europe, the United States from 1939 to 1941
became more and more the defender of Western interests in Asia. If
Great Britain lost its empire in Asia, it might well collapse in Europe,
and the British Royal Navy would no longer stand between the United
States and Germany. It is not too much to say that the Japanese were
striking every bit as much against British interests when they attacked
Pearl Harbor as they were against the United States. The two had become
inseparable in Japanese minds. The British factor in the Japanese de-

cision for war, often forgotten by Americans, is, as the British might say, rather an important one.

Roosevelt, convinced that economic pressures would induce the Japanese government to yield to America's demands, met all Japanese proposals with great firmness. It is strange that he met the situation in East Asia with directness and firmness because he did not meet the European situation in the same manner. Roosevelt's only deterrent outside of the perceived economic one—the American fleet stationed at Pearl Harbor—became important. The question of whether the fleet should remain at Pearl Harbor or return to San Diego involved a political decision as well, since the Japanese might construe an American withdrawal as a sign of weakness. Therefore the fleet remained at Pearl Harbor.

In December 1940 Roosevelt had received an important lever. Army and navy intelligence cracked the Japanese diplomatic code and then could read messages from the Japanese embassy in Washington to the Japanese foreign office in Tokyo. From these intercepts the Roosevelt administration knew the Japanese would sooner or later attempt to expand further; where, when, and against whom remained unclear until the very last. At this time the Japanese began seriously to debate the idea of a surprise attack on Pearl Harbor, but that crucial fact never surfaced in the messages.

Throughout 1941, negotiations continued between representatives of the United States and Japan. Admiral Nomura Kichisaburo, the Japanese ambassador in Washington, sincerely hoped for a peaceful settlement, but time and again the two countries disagreed on China. While Nomura carried on the negotiations, in July of 1941 the Japanese made the final formal decision that they would turn to the south; the Japanese war minister, Tojo Hideki, had converted the cabinet to his viewpoint. In that same month the Japanese landed in Indochina and prepared to attack the Dutch East Indies.

Roosevelt acted promptly. On July 25, 1941, in an extremely important step, Roosevelt issued an order to freeze all Japanese assets in the United States and imposed an embargo on all war materials, including oil. Most observers think the freezing order, a severe blow to the Jap-

Japanese Domination of the Pacific Basin, 1942

anese, was the single most crucial step taken in the entire course of Japanese-American relations before Pearl Harbor. It is uncertain that the president realized the full significance of his step. American officials believed the Japanese now had the choice of backing down or fighting. The great majority expected the Japanese to back down, and even those who thought the Japanese might fight gave them little chance in a war with the United States. Americans still hoped for a postponement of hostilities to give them time to grow even stronger. That, of course, was exactly what worried Japanese military men who preferred to fight while Japan was strong and the United States weak. All of this further increased pressures on the Japanese to move into the oil rich Dutch East Indies to get oil supplies for their war machine.

Some small degree of indecision still existed within the Japanese cabinet as Premier Konoye favored a strategic retreat; he would not abandon Japan's goals, but he would try to eliminate tension with the United States and perhaps even postpone war. Tojo's group wanted to push ahead. Konoye suggested a summit meeting with FDR in Hawaii or Alaska. Secretary of State Hull, however, wanted a general statement of principles from the Japanese before holding such a meeting. It looked to Hull, especially from the secret coded messages, that the Japanese had not changed their mind. The meeting never took place. Many of FDR's opponents have criticized him for his failure to meet with Konoye, but the Japanese premier did not dominate his cabinet, and it is extremely doubtful that the meeting could have stalled the war for more than a few months. Both governments had decided on tough, uncompromising approaches. Each felt that if only they got tough enough, the other side would back down.

On September 6 the Japanese cabinet members talked the situation over with Emperor Hirohito. While they concurred that diplomatic negotiations should continue, they also decided that if these failed the empire would undertake war with the United States, Britain, and the Netherlands. The Japanese Naval War College had already begun to practice war games simulating a December attack on Pearl Harbor. Many officers believed it could never work without detection, but Admiral Yamamoto firmly pushed his plan through and preparations moved ahead.

In October the Konoye ministry collapsed, and Tojo became premier. Tojo did not favor further negotiations, but the emperor did. Thus a special envoy, Saburo Kurusu, went to the United States to help Ambassador Nomura make one final attempt to secure Japanese demands. The Japanese offered to withdraw their troops from Indochina and China two years after the settlement of the China incident; that promise appeared much too vague to Hull. Kurusu then suggested working out a temporary settlement (*modus vivendi*) until both sides could reach a satisfactory long-term settlement. Before Hull could respond, the Japanese presented a final proposal which involved American cooperation with the Japanese to increase their supply of oil from the Netherlands and a promise to withdraw from China after peace came with Chiang. Hull rejected this approach, but he remained interested in the temporary settlement. The British, Australians, Chinese, and Dutch, however, regarded the plan as a sort of Munich, and Hull had to discard it (among its terms: a three months' truce, the withdrawal of Japanese troops from Indochina, no further military advances by Japan, and the United States to resume full trade with the Japanese). Hull on November 26 countered with an American ten-point program that would settle the dispute strictly along American lines. Apparently convinced of the impossibility of concessions, Hull returned to his firm line.

Japan's response, of course, came on the morning of December 7, 1941. The Japanese fleet, six new aircraft carriers protected by twenty-five other ships, had left the Japanese islands on November 26 for a long trip across the Pacific. The disaster that occurred at Pearl Harbor stemmed from the bad judgment of the Roosevelt administration, a failure to evaluate intelligence information properly, and sheer administrative negligence. The administration did not expect the attack at Pearl Harbor, but it did expect an attack by the Japanese to come somewhere in Southeast Asia and did not warn the Pearl Harbor commanders of the seriousness of the diplomatic situation. And there were those, after all, such as Major George Fielding Elliot, who wrote in 1938 that "a Japanese attack on Pearl Harbor is a strategic impossibility." Pearl Harbor's military commanders prepared thus for sabotage but not for an attack. For example, they parked all the airplanes together in the center of the field to make sabotage harder and guard work easier; such a procedure made it possible for Japanese attackers to destroy many American planes with one bomb. The lack of precautionary measures taken at Pearl Harbor reflects as badly on the Roosevelt administration as on the commanders on the spot.

While it is indeed true, as mentioned, that military intelligence had broken Japanese codes and could intercept and read Japanese diplomatic messages, even with ingenious machines interception and decoding remained a complicated and slow process that in the final analysis depended on human beings to interpret the information. In addition, Hawaii did not have one of the machines, and American commanders as a result had no access to the "Magic" messages. None of the messages indicated precisely when and where the attack would come except for one of December 6 not fully decoded until December 8. Some indications in previous messages had somewhat pointed to Pearl Harbor when the Japanese asked their agents there to keep track of all ship movements. And at 11:15 (about two hours prior to the attack) a message went to the White House reporting the destruction of code books at the Japanese embassy and that the Japanese ambassadors would present Japan's answer at 1:00 that afternoon. General Marshall then sent out an alert, but it did not reach Pearl Harbor until after the attack had started.

President Roosevelt appeared before Congress the next day and described the Japanese strike as a "date which will live in infamy." The House declared war on Japan by a vote of 388-1 and the Senate followed with a unanimous vote.

On December 11 Hitler asked the German Reichstag for a declaration of war on the United States; in the process he accused Roosevelt of being "Mad, just as Wilson was." Not informed by the Japanese of the attack prior to its actuality, Hitler believed that a state of war had in fact existed between Germany and the United States since Roosevelt has issued the shoot-on-sight order on September 11. Hitler said that "a great power like Germany declares war, it does not wait until somebody else declares it." Under no obligation to declare war under any of the Axis pacts, he took this crucial step at the same time that his armies were stalling before the gates of Moscow. The United States in return declared war on Germany and Italy on the same day.

If war with Germany was indeed a strong possibility, and Americans and Germans in fact were killing each other in the North Atlantic in the winter of 1941–1942, might it not have been greater wisdom and statesmanship to have negotiated a temporary settlement with the Japanese government in the fall of 1941? The Roosevelt administration always viewed Germany, both prior to and during the war, as the far more important and dangerous foe. A temporary truce with the Japanese would have permitted the American arsenal of democracy to have sent far more supplies and men to the aid of the Allies, and might well have brought about the defeat of the Germans one or more years earlier. An earlier German defeat would not only have saved lives but might also have brought about a different postwar settlement in Europe. Both American and Russian forces would, in all probability, have occupied different territories than they actually did and a more advantageous political situation might have prevailed. At the end of the war with Germany, the entire coalition could have turned against the Japanese and demanded their withdrawal from China and Southeast Asia. The Japanese could not have refused. The dropping of the atomic bombs might well have proved unnecessary. Statesmanship, above all, involves an ordering of priorities. A two-year truce with the Japanese, impossible of course after Pearl Harbor, would not have directly threatened American interests.

A political scientist, Bruce Russett, goes beyond even this suggestion and argues in his book *No Clear and Present Danger* that "American participation in World War II brought the country few gains; the United States was no more secure at the end that it could have been had it stayed out." He also finds that "In cold-blooded realist terms, Nazism as an ideology was almost certainly less dangerous to the United States than is Communism." Russett's conclusions cannot, however, diminish the perception of the American government in 1941 that Germany was *the* threat. Perceptions, true and false, have as much to do with a nation's history as do "real facts" and "truth."

Did Nazi Germany present a threat to the United States? Moral repugnancy? Clearly. A threat? Less clear, but certainly discernible. German submarines had fired on American fighting ships, not just merchant ships, and Americans had died. The United States had gone to war twice, in 1812 and in 1917, in the face of similar provocations.

Churchill certainly believed in the fall of 1941 that the American president had told him that he, Roosevelt, hoped to find an incident to justify opening hostilities against Nazi Germany. Even if a historian assumes elements of wishful thinking in Churchill's report, he will search in vain for a statement in 1941 by the president that the United States would not go to war against Germany. Regardless of how the war turned out, the Roosevelt administration in 1941 clearly perceived Germany as a threat, and had put the United States on the road to war with Germany, probably in early 1942.

Selected Reading

On American entrance into the Second World War the two-volume work by William L. Langer and S. Everett Gleason, *The Challenge to Isolation, 1937–1940* (1952) and *The Undeclared War, 1940–1941* (1953) remains the most comprehensive history. John Wiltz's *From Isolation to War, 1931–1941* (1968) is a good brief introduction. A careful work by Wayne S. Cole, *Roosevelt and the Isolationists 1932–1945* (1983) can be supplemented by James Patterson, *Mr. Republican: A Biography of Robert A. Taft* (1972) and Manfred Jonas *Isolationism in America, 1935–41* (1966).

The *Approach to War, 1938–1939* (1967) by Christopher Thorne is strong and provocative on the European background of the war, as is A.J.P. Taylor in his *The Origins of the Second World War*, 2nd ed. (1961). J.W. Wheeler-Bennett's *Munich: Prologue to Tragedy* (1948) is a forgotten classic. Saul Friedlander's *Prelude to Downfall: Hitler and the United States, 1939–1941* (1967), William E. Kinsella, Jr.'s *Leadership in Isolation: FDR and the Origins of the Second World War* (1978), and T.R. Fehrenbach's *F.D.R.'s Undeclared War: 1939–1941* (1967) concentrate on the European road to war.

The road to war with Japan is best covered in Waldo H. Heinrichs, Jr., *American Ambassador: Joseph C. Grew and the Development of the United States Diplomatic Tradition* (1966) and the overwhelming *Pearl Harbor as History: Japanese-American Relations, 1931–1941* (1973), edited by Dorothy Borg and Shumpei Okamoto. The best recent work is the important *Going to War with Japan, 1937–1941* (1985) by Jonathan G. Utley—a model monograph. Ian Nish, ed., *Anglo-Japanese Alienation, 1919–1952* (1952) places heavy responsibilities on the United States. *Race to Pearl Harbor: The Failure of the Second London Naval Conference and the Onset of World War II* (1974) by Stephen Pelz adds the naval perspective. Volumes by Robert Butow on *Tojo and the Coming of the War* (1961) and *The John Doe Associates: Backdoor Diplomacy for Peace* (1974) present important aspects of the diplomatic negotiations as does James Herzog in *Closing the Open Door: American-Japanese*

Diplomatic Negotiations, 1936–1941 (1973). John J. Stephen's recent book, *Hawaii Under the Rising Sun: Japan's Plans for Conquest After Pearl Harbor* (1984) is important and revealing.

Pearl Harbor materials are voluminous. Walter Millis' *This is Pearl!* (1947) captures the tragic drama of the event better than anyone. Gordon Prange's monumental *At Dawn We Slept* (1981) coupled with his *Pearl Harbor: The Verdict of History* (1985) present the most comprehensive story of the attack and its interpretations. *Pearl Harbor: Warning and Decision* (1962) by Roberta Wohlstetter concentrates on the "Magic" intercepted messages. Revisionist works placing major responsibility on FDR, such as Charles Tansill's *Back Door to War: The Roosevelt Foreign Policy, 1933–1941* (1952) and John Toland's *Infamy: Pearl Harbor and Its Aftermath* (1982), have not convinced many historians.

Bruce Russett in *No Clear and Present Danger: A Skeptical View of the United States Entry Into World War II* (1972) briefly argues against going into the war at all. And John J. Mearsheimer's *Conventional Deterrence* (1983) and Alexander L. George and Richard Smoke's *Deterrence in American Foreign Policy: Theory and Practice* (1974) raise interesting theoretical questions.

Latin America and the Transformation of U.S. Strategic Thought, 1936–1940 (1984) by David G. Haglund presents an illuminating argument placing Latin America at the center of the strategic debate.

8 Second World War

Americans have long reveled in their reputation as a nation of achievers. The Second World War confirmed both the strength and weakness of that claim. One writer has compared the United States to a sleeping dinosaur—a monster of enormous strength, minding its own business, quietly dozing while various smaller, weaker creatures peck at it here and there; some intruders leave deposits around on it, still others walk right over it, but, when finally angered, the dinosaur rises and destroys everything in sight as efficiently and as quickly as possible. The dinosaur cures the immediate problem without concern about other problems its actions create. In a similar manner, born of a desire to bring a speedy end to the war, and thereby save American lives, the United States and its allies militarily defeated the Germans in 41 months and the Japanese in 45. Overwhelming military success, however, was not matched by comparable political achievement.

Historian Michael Howard, a close student of the writings of Carl von Clausewitz, suggests that wars are fought for particular reasons to achieve specific goals. Once the question of a nation's survival is determined, and survival was probably never at stake in the American case, then political goals become more important than military ones. A country does not simply want to defeat its enemies in a military sense, but also to gain as much security for the future as possible. Enemies are not like climbing mountains, fought only because they are there. The lives of tens of thousands of men and billions of dollars are used either to prevent that particular war from reoccurring or to build obstacles against another nation replacing the defeated enemy and presenting a **169** similar challenge. Such considerations did not enter the American consciousness. Deliberate postponement of political settlements by the Roosevelt administration, following the pattern of Woodrow Wilson during the First World War, meant that the postwar arrangements would largely depend on one or both of two factors: 1) what territory each country's military occupied or controlled on the day the war ended; and 2) what terms each country could win at the peace conference to protect its interests. Since the conference never met, the former became the determining factor of the postwar settlement. No country played the political game as well as the Soviet Union, few played it as badly as the United States.

Reasons, of course, existed for the postponement of political decisions. Foremost was the underlying level of suspicion among the three powers—the United States, Great Britain, and the Soviet Union. Stalin, on his part, feared that the Western allies would let the Germans devastate Russia to the point of Soviet exhaustion before committing troops to a second front. Churchill and Roosevelt, on their part, remembering the Russian separate peace with Germany in 1918 and the Nazi-Soviet pact of 1939, feared a third Soviet-German deal that would leave the Western Powers facing Hitler, as well as the Japanese, by themselves. By subordinating political concerns and concentrating on the military defeat of first Germany and then Japan, perhaps the political problems of an alliance with the Soviet Union, whose leaders, after all, had called again and again for the overthrow of capitalist countries, could be overcome and settlements made after winning the friendship of the Soviets.

Churchill appeared more willing to face the Russian problem earlier than Roosevelt, who is reported to have said that "Stalin doesn't want anything but security for his country. I think that if I give him everything I possibly can and ask for nothing in return, he won't try to annex anything and will work with me for a world of peace and democracy." Putting aside the fact the Roosevelt surely recognized that Stalin's definitions of both "peace and democracy" differed from his, the president's reputation for political realism is not enhanced. Even as late as April 11, 1945, the day before his death, FDR wrote Churchill that he "would minimize the general Soviet problems as much as possible, because these problems, in one form or another, seem to arise every day and most of them straighten out." A large element of wishful thinking, indeed of gambling, is present. Roosevelt forgot the wise advice of George Washington that "no nation is to be trusted further than it is bound by its interest; and no prudent statesman or politician will venture to depart from it."

What, then, appears to have been the political and economic goals of the great powers other than the military defeat of the Germans and Japanese? The Roosevelt administration reflected the belief of most Americans that a world composed of democratic, capitalistic nations offered not only the best chance for peace but also the greatest opportunity for American institutions to thrive and grow. There were, however, Americans such as Herman Wells, the president of Indiana University, who warned "We should not seek to place a union building on every campus in China, a juke box in every Eskimo's igloo, or two cars in every Hottentot's garage. There are able men and women in every land, capable of developing a society as satisfactory to them as ours is to us." But this time, unlike the First World War, the total defeat and occupation of Germany would bring home to the Germans the error of their warlike ways. The United States would not return to its prewar isolationism nor would it enter into a balance of power arrangement or agree to spheres of influence. Rather, the peace would involve cooperation, not competition, between the great powers. Roosevelt's "Four Policemen"—the United States, Great Britain, Russia, and China—would have a monopoly of military power and collectively establish political arrangements based on mutual trust and reciprocity. Permanent troop dispositions by the United States in either Europe or Asia were not envisioned or desired by the president. FDR, clearly not as idealistic about collective security as Wilson, came late to the United Nations idea and in effect accepted the concept of a security council as more of a cover, instead of a substitute, for the Four Policemen. The president gambled that the Soviet Union would show restraint in its security demands, that China would become a great power in fact as well as in name, and that Great Britain would show an example for others by voluntarily breaking up its colonial empire. A trusteeship for Indochina, then under French rule, might also serve as an example of how empires were to be broken up. In the area of economics he pushed for a free

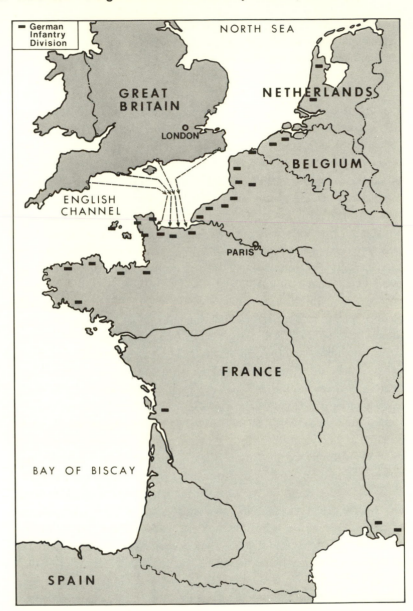

The Allied Invasion, June 6, 1944

trade world in which the powerful American economy, undevastated by war, would certainly have an initial, if not permanent, advantage. These, more in terms of general principles than in specifics, were the goals the president hoped to achieve for this country.

Churchill, on the other hand, wanted to preserve Great Britain's position as a great power. While he would accept the notion of giving increased self-government to colonies, he had no intention of abandoning the British Empire. The prime minister still believed that Europe would remain the center of world politics; its fate would still determine the future of the world. Not antagonistic to balance of power politics, or to the creation of spheres of influence, he hoped that the United States would remain in Europe and help rebuild a balance of power that would openly deal with what he perceived to be a basic conflict of interest with the Soviet Union. Rather than punishing Germany he would work to create a nonmilitarized, democratic nation that could contribute to the overall strength of Europe. He found it difficult to accept Roosevelt's promotion of China to the status of world power, and found it hard to differentiate between that American goal and the American desire to push Great Britain out of its Asian possessions. Churchill saw things in the classic British manner, but he realized that Great Britain could only keep its world power status in cooperation with the United States. Great Britain no longer had the power to act alone, and this became clearer and clearer with each passing year of the war. Not even Churchill's great strength, vigorous sense of purpose, and courage could overcome that obstacle.

Roosevelt and Churchill had a close but not always harmonious, relationship. While the prime minister stressed the closeness in his memoirs, there were in fact serious strains. Most of the disputes arose not over the fighting of the war, but over the shape of the postwar world. FDR, for example, wanted American civil aviation to have a crack at the world market in an open competition, while Churchill preferred a pooling arrangement. When the president later threatened to cut off lend-lease, Churchill, by 1944 the junior partner, could only plead for mercy. As the publication of the full Roosevelt-Churchill correspondence reveals, in Alistar Horne's words, Roosevelt "comes across as cold, concise, businesslike and often devious; Churchill as the emotional romantic, always the literary figure, often taurine, but perhaps less Machiavellian." Despite such differences in personality and outlook, concentration on the disputes should not obscure the essential cooperation between the leaders and their countries. Seldom in history have two allies fought together so successfully. What made it possible, however, was the increasing British willingness to accept a subordinate position to the United States.

The Soviet Union, represented by Stalin, muted its communist international stridency and stressed Russian nationalism. While this masked its ultimate goals, at the least Western leaders could have counted on the Soviet Union pursuing many of the same goals as Imperial Tsarist Russia—acquisition of ice-free ports, control of the Dardanelles (the strait between Turkey and Russia commanding the entrance and exit to the Black Sea), and the creation of a series of buffer states in Eastern Europe and Asia. Russia, Tsarist or Soviet, after all, was not the largest country in the world in land mass, due to a lack of attention by its rulers, for whatever reasons, to continental expansion. While it is extremely doubtful that Stalin had a plan for worldwide domination, it is likely that he was opportunistic and willing to take advantage of openings offered by the developing situation. He would have been a fool to ignore them, and Stalin, ruthless and perhaps paranoid, was not a fool. Certainly Germany was the key, and the prevention of its return to power was a primary goal of Soviet policy. Stalin said little about the Asian situation, but even there pursued the same goals as Tsarist Russia. A tough and capable negotiator, "Uncle Joe," as Roosevelt called him, was in the struggle for the long-run and used Russia's favorable geographical position and abundant military forces to gain political ends.

China's situation was the weakest of the four powers. Chiang Kai-shek's nation was torn by not only the Japanese invasion but the threat of a civil war between Chiang's Nationalists and Mao Tse-tung's Communists. China's destiny clearly lay in the future, but its present troubles were an irritant within the coalition. Only the United States treated the Chinese like representatives of a world power. Both the Russians and British viewed China primarily as an American protégé. Chiang, of course, wanted a bigger role. But internal corruption, inflation, and plain military incompetence robbed his regime not only of its claims but, in time, of its existence. He hoped to keep China in one territorial piece, build up enough military power to defeat the Communists, and gain economic aid from the United States. He did succeed in the classical Chinese policy of playing the great powers off against each other, which preserved almost all of China's lands. Nonetheless Chiang failed to either build up or use his military strength wisely, and he successfully gained American aid only to squander it. Roosevelt, almost to the last, refused to tie strings to the aid. Nowhere did the eternal gap between American hopes and what actually happened end up as wide as it did in China—in part, it must be noted, because the goals were impossible to achieve with available American power.

If there were clearly strains within the alliance, it must always be remembered that Axis diplomacy and military cooperation were among the greatest assets the Allied cause possessed. As previously noted, had the Japanese invaded Siberia at the same time in 1941, the very existence of the Soviet regime might well have been at stake. If the Germans had not forewarned the Japanese of either the Nazi-Soviet pact of 1939 or the invasion of Russian in 1941, the Japanese returned the favor by not informing the Germans of the Pearl Harbor attack. A closer cooperation between the Japanese and Germans—suppose, for example, the Japanese had created a ring of buffer states in Southeast Asia to link up with the German and Italian areas in the Near and Middle East—would have made Allied prosecution of the war much more difficult. Hitler and Mussolini very much wanted the Japanese to send their naval forces into the Indian Ocean to threaten and attack the key British supply lines. A statement by Hitler in late 1939 indicates part of the problem: "Let us think of ourselves as masters and consider these people [the Japanese] at best as lacquered half-monkeys, who need to feel the knout." Fortunately for the Allies, such racist sentiments, not unknown to the Japanese, made cooperation, even given wartime pressures, all but impossible.

The Japanese, in particular, gave almost no thought whatsoever to long-term planning either in the military or political sphere. They expected the United States to accept the loss of the western Pacific as final and as too costly to regain, and to seek a negotiated peace. It was not until after Pearl Harbor that they even realized that they could have invaded and occupied Hawaii. Not only those short-term plans, but others, went into the scrap barrel with the American victory at Midway in June 1942, which took the strategic initiative away from the Japanese. As the Americans and British began to push toward Japan through the Pacific islands, the Japanese, fearful of a Russian attack, retained in Manchuria thirteen to fifteen divisions whose presence in the islands might well have stalled the Allied drive and at the least have made it far more costly. Overconfidence, the result of easy early victories, was certainly a factor. Finally, there was little consideration given to building up a defensive ring against the inevitable Allied attempt to regain their position. Japan, even more vulnerable than Great Britain to maritime war against its import needs, did not spend much time devising convoy protection, anti-submarine warfare, or other techniques to keep the logistical lines open and operating. The result was slow but sure strangling of Japanese supplies as American naval and air power closed their own ring around Japan with the conquest of each island group.

Each of the Allied Powers followed a different approach to fighting the war; that process revealed much about each society. The Americans depended on a massing of economic power, a mechanization of war, an emphasis on air power, and a downgrading of total infantry power, of actual troops on the ground.

Mobilization during the Second World War had distinctive American characteristics. Spared from both bombing and invasion, American society in general and American manpower in particular were less mobilized for strictly military purposes than those of any other major belligerent. Despite the shift of most heavy industry to wartime production, most light industry, which employed the majority of American workers, continued to produce civilian products. American society in general did not greatly suffer, and large segments of the population prospered. A surprisingly small proportion of the society were direct participants in either war industries or frontline warfare, for American mobilization was based more on an "arsenal of democracy" basis than on an "arsenal of manpower." Ships, shells, tanks, trucks, and airplanes from the United States were used by all the Allied combatants, but far fewer soldiers appeared in the front lines. The size of the American military was thus much smaller than that, for example, of the Soviet

Nine huge liberty ships at outfitting dock of California Shipbuilding Corps, 1943

Union. And, as well, noncombatant support groups made up a larger proportion of the American military; war was thought of in management terms as much as in fighting terms. The American concentration on airpower, rather than on infantry troops, was in part a reflection of the belief that an abundance of high firepower weapons, based on an application of technology, would spare the United States high human casualty rates.

The British, too, were beguiled by the genie of air power and also did not have a large number of ground troops; too many memories of miles of white crosses in military cemeteries of the First World War remained vividly etched in their minds. The Red Army, however, depended, as always in Russian history, on large numbers of land troops and increasing numbers of tanks. When the war ended, the Soviets had the world's largest army in place on the borderlands of Western Europe. The Red Army's logistics system was interesting: for example, the Soviets used horsedrawn wooden carts to get artillery shells to the front over axle-deep mud or snow. The carts used no gasoline, and at the front the artillery shells would be fired off, the carts would be broken up for firewood, the horses eaten, and the drivers put into the frontline. No deadheading, no waste. The Chinese army, while also large in total numbers, had a command structure in which loyalty to Chiang was more important than the military ability of the general. Therefore few generals wanted to risk their position by risking defeat; it was easier to avoid battle with the Japanese and attempt to accumulate wealth. For this reason most Chinese troops, almost all conscripts, were underfed, badly trained, poorly equipped, and unenthusiastic because their officers cared little about their welfare.

Stalin wanted a second front launched as soon as possible to draw off German troops massed within Russia and pressing on Moscow and Stalingrad. Roosevelt incautiously promised one by the end of 1942. Had it taken place then there is a good chance that the Germans would have thrown the Allies back into the sea. Fortunately the British recognized this and refused to support the American proposal. The final result was a compromise that led to the invasion in North Africa. This did not please Stalin, and the Russians continued to bear the major burden against the bulk of the German army.

The question of where the landings were to take place in Europe generated controversy both then and later. American military leaders favored a cross-channel attack against the coast of France, launched from the secure base of the British islands. While accepting the American concept of a powerful knockout punch, a boxing term that seemed to envision a Joe Louis military destroying a Max Schmeling opponent with a quick count in the first round, the British wanted to risk as few of their soldiers as possible. They could not afford another First World War "victory." A Balkan invasion through what Churchill called the "soft under-belly" of Europe, first suggested by Roosevelt as one alternative, was therefore eagerly picked up and supported by the prime minister. It has been argued that had the Western Allies driven into the Balkans, their troops, not Russian ones, would have occupied the major capitals of Eastern Europe and prevented the Russian takeover of that area. William Bullitt, one of FDR's foreign policy advisers, in 1943 warned of the Soviet plans and said, "Stalin like Hitler will not stop. He can only be stopped." Bullitt called for the "barring to the Red Army of the way into Europe."

While an interesting theory, it had basic faults in fact. A segment of the British proposal, but not with the major forces that invaded Normandy, did take place with the landings in Sicily, Italy, and later ones in southern France. As American General Mark Clark pointed out, based on the hard fighting in Italy where German artillery in the mountains successfully tied down large numbers of Allied troops, the soft under-belly was a "tough old gut." It is quite possible that in the even more inhospitable terrain of the southern Balkans the Allied armies might have similarly stalled. Russian armies might have pushed even further across the northern plains to take all of Germany and part of France. Both, in a political power sense, were more valuable than Eastern Europe.

The Normandy campaign itself, contrary to popular myth, was not a succession of easy victories against a weakened foe. There are those to this day who argue that the German army was the best fighting force of the Second World War and that its extraordinary skills were only blunted by the superior air power of the Allies, a final exhaustion, and poor direction by Hitler. Allied casualties were high; again and again outnumbered German troops with superior technology held off, stalled, and sometimes pushed back the Allies. The Second World War in Europe was much more of a near thing than most realize. Had Hitler had more submarines, invaded Russia earlier in the spring (with a concurrent Japanese invasion), perfected the jet plane and missile and produced them in greater quantities, and finally pushed harder on the development of the atomic bomb, the difficulties of the Allies would have increased dramatically.

The demand for unconditional surrender of the Axis Powers, while understandable and intended to prevent a reoccurrence of the stab-in-the-back theory used by Hitler in the 1920s and 1930s to explain to Germans that Germany had not really lost the First World War in a military sense, had mixed results. With regard to Germany there is some

evidence that the German leaders effectively used the threat of unconditional surrender to encourage their people and military to fight longer
because a negotiated peace was not permitted. On the other hand it is
also true that a negotiated settlement with Hitler was impossible because
of the evil he represented. There were Germans who wanted peace, and
several plots against Hitler's life took place. One, a bomb explosion in
a wooden building above ground that dissipated the blast effects, almost
succeeded; had the meeting taken place as scheduled in an underground
concrete bunker, Hitler would not have survived. Nevertheless, the fact
is that Hitler's orders were still being obeyed until the last hours of his
life. On balance, those who argue that the policy was wise toward
Germany have a good case.

Japan, however, represents a different situation. It can be argued
that the Japanese might well have been negotiated out of the war. The
responsibility for the fact that it did not happen is a shared one. Americans wanted to punish the Japanese and in particular were unwilling
initially to accept any arrangement that would leave the emperor on the
throne. While the emperor was finally allowed to remain as a symbol,
there was not a clear signal of this to the Japanese until after the atomic
bombs were dropped. An earlier indication might well have influenced
the Japanese government, and in particular the emperor, to overcome
those in the military who wanted to fight to the bitter end. Those who
wanted to continue the struggle were strong. The Japanese government,
largely using the Soviet Union as an intermediary, also had put out
peace feelers; the vagueness and weakness of the proposals did not
encourage response. It has proven much more difficult to end wars in
the twentieth century than it has been to start them. In this specific case,
both sides were closer to agreement than either realized, but both failed
to communicate properly. Application of the unconditional surrender
doctrine to Japan raised an unnecessary hurdle that led directly to the
dropping of the atomic bombs.

In the realm of naval strategy the specific application of Mahan's
battle theories did not work out in the Second World War. The question
of command of the seas was not settled by decisive big battles either
at Jutland during the First World War or at Midway during the Second.
Nor did the capital ship prove its overwhelming superiority. Even the

new capital ship of the 1940s, the aircraft carrier, which replaced the battleship, proved a double-edged sword. For while carrier planes could seek out and destroy other ships, the carrier itself was vulnerable to similar applications of airpower. An overenthusiastic airforce general, James Doolittle, by 1946 was labeling carriers obsolete in an era of air power. More important, Mahan strategists continued to ignore an even more fatal flaw in his strategic thinking. Twice in this century submarine warfare has almost cut the sea lines of communication: German U-boats had great success against Allied shipping in the North Atlantic, and similar results were achieved by American submarines against Japanese shipping in the Pacific. Contrary to Mahan's principles, this secondary, supposedly inclusive, method of warfare, practiced against commerce and supply ships rather than capital ships, came perilously close to driving Great Britain to the wall in both wars. Only the belated adoption of convoying saved the day on both occasions. Convoy escorts not only shepherded the troop and supply ships safely across, but actually sank more submarines than the special hunter/killer groups formed to find and destroy submarines. Modern land and air warfare consumes supplies and equipment at ever increasing rates, making logistical resupply the key to modern conventional war. The Mahanites concentration on big decisive battles and capital ships ignored the importance of resupply to such a degree that only the spectacle of hundreds of ships sinking caused the navies to make belated efforts in both wars in an area that should have been a primary concern in the first place.

With respect to strategic bombing, one must note that while it is true that German war production was still going up by the summer of 1944, bombing raids on German transportation networks had been so successful that it had become extraordinarily difficult for the Germans to transport an aircraft engine produced in one factory to another location to be matched up with the aircraft frame. Further, *The United States Strategic Bombing Survey Report* notes that of all the tonnage dropped, 72 percent was dropped on Germany after July 1, 1944. The gradual implementation of the bombing campaign has led some critics to concentrate on the period prior to July 1944 and to label strategic bombing a total failure. A more balanced assessment would find both successes (transportation facilities and oil supplies destroyed) as well as failures (population

Wurtzburg, Germany, 1945. The famous university town was heavily bombed because of its important industrial plants and railway lines.

centers bombed with high civilian casualities and industrial production not critically affected prior to July 1944). Bombing in general was much more successful after that date. The controversy over both the effectiveness and morality of strategic bombing, however, has continued to the present day.

The famous Yalta Conference in February 1945 confirmed decisions made at the previous wartime conference among the great powers. Later charges of betrayal raised by conservatives and Republican opposition leaders are not supported by what actually took place. Voting arrangements in the proposed United Nations, the potential use of the veto in that organization, the formation of occupation zones in Germany, the Russian statement that they would enter the war against Japan within ninety days of the end of the struggle with Germany (in return for economic and political concessions in Manchuria and the Pacific), and a promise to support free elections in liberated Europe were the major decisions that resulted from Yalta. Roosevelt, tired and wan, was to die within six weeks of his return from the conference. Neither the president's intellectual powers nor his concentration were at their peak. He seldom read the briefing books and materials prepared for him. But to jump to a conclusion that Roosevelt deviated from previous American policies to give the Soviet Union advantages is unwarranted.

Stalin's promise to support free elections in the soon to be liberated countries of Europe, however, might have been suspect after his handling of Poland. Poles and Russians had been at each others' throats for centuries; neither had much historical reason to accept the words of the other, no matter how democratically phrased. Thus when the Soviet armies were about fifty miles from Warsaw in August of 1944, the Polish leadership in the city called for an uprising against their German military occupiers. They hoped to free the city before the Russians arrived and have an operating Polish government in place. *Jeszcze Polska nie zginela,* "Poland is not yet lost," the opening words of the Polish national anthem, filled the air. Unfortunately, after the uprising began, the Russian armies stopped; the Germans poured in reinforcements and crushed the revolt. After the Germans had wiped out the Polish fighters, who would have opposed Russian overlordship as strongly as they had opposed German rule, the Russian armies started up again and took

Warsaw in January 1945. Some 85 percent of the city was destroyed, and over half of its prewar population was dead. Churchill was to ask Roosevelt about two weeks prior to FDR's death, "Surely we must not be maneuvered into becoming parties to imposing on Poland, and how much of Eastern Europe, the Russian version of democracy?" The massive size of the Soviet land forces and their position, already in actual control of much of the borderlands, would determine the fate of Eastern Europe. Stalin's promise was all that Roosevelt felt he could get under the circumstances, unless he meant to openly challenge the Soviet Union. By Yalta the president had neither the strength nor the will to do so, but Churchill, who at an earlier time had been willing to hand over the Baltic States and eastern Poland to Stalin, was now calling for a stronger line against the Soviets.

Equally puzzling is the record of the Roosevelt administration on its "abandonment of the Jews" to the horrors of Nazi persecution. While it is true that hard facts were unavailable until November 1942, it is also true that neither the president nor the Department of State exhibited anything but indifference toward a host of rumors about the existence of the death camps. Author David S. Wyman argues that "Roosevelts' indifference to so momentous and historical event as the systematic annihilation of European Jewry emerges as the worst failure of his presidency." For example, while 190,000 Jews could have legally found refuge in the United States under the immigration quotas from 1941 to 1945, only 21,000 actually were allowed to enter. Public opinion, infused with anti-Semitic, anti-immigration feelings, as well as residues from the great unemployment of the 1930s, did not subject the administration to either moral or political pressure. Historians have not found real desire on the part of large numbers of organized Americans to rescue the Jews as Roosevelt waited fourteen months after November 1942 to establish a War Refugee Board in 1944. The president, as mentioned, rarely put his real thoughts on paper, so we will never know his true thoughts on this issue, but for a man whose reputation as a great humanitarian rings through history books, his failure to act is at best puzzling, at worst perhaps a reflection of American society.

Roosevelt died in April 1945, so it was not Roosevelt but the new president, Harry Truman, who attended the last wartime conference at

Potsdam. Truman, inexperienced in foreign affairs, met with the new British leader, Clement Atlee, who replaced Churchill in mid-conference. The Potsdam Declaration warned Japan that it faced "prompt and utter destruction" unless it surrendered immediately. The Japanese, in a world-changing decision, did not accept until it was too late.

The dropping of atomic bombs on Japan remains both a political and moral dispute forty years after the event. Fear of Germany acquiring the bomb before the allies was the initial impetus for the development program. Fortunately the Germans failed, and a Japanese program was even less far along as the war ended. But the Russians, helped by the spy Klaus Fuchs, were well along the road to success. Interestingly enough, on March 10, 1945, the Japanese inadvertently almost literally short-circuited the American program. A Japanese paper balloon, one of thousands launched from Japan with incendiary bombs aboard, dropped in the Hanford, Washington, area, hit power lines, and caused a power failure that almost caused the nearby secret nuclear reactors to shut down. If untested safety procedures had not worked, the first nuclear explosion might well have occurred at that time in a calamitous disaster. The only certainty of history remains uncertainty.

Nevertheless the United States was preparing to test its new weapon by the summer of 1945, and the question of whether it should be used against Japan arose. As Allied troops approached the main islands, the fighting in such island outposts as Iwo Jima and Okinawa became increasingly more difficult and costly in human lives. No one had successfully invaded Japan in its entire history. Two huge invasions by the Mongols led by Kublai Khan in 1271 and 1274 had failed not only because of Japanese fighting skills but because of typhoons, called divine winds or *kamikaze,* coming up both times and helping to destroy the Mongol fleets. Knowing that the Americans would probably not be well mannered enough to attack during similar typhoons, the Japanese began to produce kamikaze suicide airplanes to take the place of the typhoons. Many American ships, including aircraft carriers, were heavily damaged or sunk by the planes; an effective weapon, hundreds more were being readied. Estimates of the human cost in fighting the Japanese on their home ground ranged from 500,000 to 1,000,000 Americans, although recent estimates by historians, assisted by fuller information than Truman

**Occupied by
Russian Forces**

Aug./Dec. 1944

Dec. 1945/
Apr. 1945

FINLAND

HELSINKI

LENINGRAD

TALLINN

BALTIC
SEA

ESTONIA

PSKOV

LATVIA

LITHUANIA

KONINGSBERG

KAUNAS

MINSK

EAST
PRUSSIA

BIALYSTOK

BERLIN

WARSAW

GERMANY

POLAND

KIEV

PRAGUE

KRAKOW

LVOV

CZECHOSLOVAKIA

VIENNA

BUDAPEST

HUNGARY

ODESSA

RUMANIA

BELGRADE

BUCHAREST

YUGOSLAVIA

BULGARIA

The Eastern Front, 1945

had available to him, place the figure at less than 50,000. B-29 fire bomb raids, under the direction of U.S. Air Force General Curtis LeMay, were already turning Japanese cities, constructed largely of wood, into raging infernos that killed more people than the atomic bombs; the Tokyo raid of March 9, 1945, killed at least 120,000 Japanese, perhaps even more. It was felt that Russian aid might be necessary in such an invasion, and a deal was negotiated returning to the Soviet Union the territories lost by Tsarist Russia in 1905 if they would enter the war against Japan. Almost every objective outward sign pointed to a bitter, bloody struggle to conquer Japan by invasion. What is often forgotten is that the cost in Japanese lives from conventional warfare and starvation might well have been also in the hundreds of thousands or more.

Scientists working on the bomb asked that a demonstration be given to the Japanese prior to using it on the home islands. President Truman did not approve, in part because there were still those who believed the bomb would not work; even Robert Oppenheimer had such fears up to the moment the first test was successful in New Mexico. But perhaps more important, there is nothing in the record to indicate that Truman ever seriously considered *not* dropping the bomb. It would save American lives and that was enough for the president. A warning was sent to Japan from Potsdam on August 2. Within twelve days the first bomb was dropped on Hiroshima, Russia declared war, a second bomb was dropped on Nagasaki, and the war ended on August 14, 1945. The Second World War had ended in clear victory for the allies.

Charges that Truman dropped the bomb not primarily to defeat Japan, but to impress and warn the Soviet Union of American power, remain interesting but unproven. Realists might well approve such a purpose but find little evidence that Truman actually acted or thought in terms so starkingly strategic and political. Two years later the president, more experienced, might well have come to such an approach, but in the summer of 1945 Truman had not yet developed the decisive attitudes that led to his metamorphosis as a cold warrior. One does not have to be a believer in conspiracy theories to accept the charge; one does, however, have to find more historical evidence that the revisionists have so far produced.

During the Second World War a partnership began to develop between soldiers and scientists, not only in the field of atomic energy, but in electronics, early forms of computers, and missiles. Bargains were made that were to support the very foundation of the development of a military/industrial complex. Scientists, previously largely ignored in the corridors of power as well as, in their own minds, undersupported in their research, suddenly found themselves important, with access to large funds. They liked it. The historian Michael Sherry best describes the process: "Scientists did not drift aimlessly into military research, nor were they duped into it. They espoused its virtues, lobbied hard for it, and rarely questioned it." Connections between major university centers of science and the military dramatically increased. By 1948, for example, the Office of Naval Research was funding no less than 896 projects at 223 universities and other research centers. Disdainful of ordinary politics, convinced that "science" was superior to its mundane concerns, ignorant in large part, or so it appears, of the moral implications of their actions, scientists inextricably linked themselves to both the military and the government. From Einstein's letter to FDR suggesting work on an atomic weapon to the "Star Wars" project of the 1980s, the progression is clear and direct.

In another area of wartime planning John McAuley Palmer and George C. Marshall came together again in 1941. Both remembered the failure to secure universal military training in 1920 and the resultant Dark Ages of the interwar period when the army received low levels of budgetary support. Competing with the navy for scarce funds, the army remained underfunded even with the rise of Germany and Japan in the 1930s, and was unprepared to meet these challenges. Both Palmer and Marshall were determined that such a sequence of events should not happen again. The goal of future peacetime preparedness should be secured prior to the end of the Second World War. Secretary of War Henry Stimson endorsed the goal of universal military training, as did Franklin Roosevelt. But, with his ultimate ends cloaked as ever, FDR then left the details up in the air. His successor, Harry Truman, with the directness for which he was to become famed, came out in public support of universal military training on October 23, 1945. For the moment it looked as if the Palmer-Marshall dream might become reality. But the proposal stalled in Congress, the self-confident air force, expecting the

Aftermath of casualties and destruction following the savage battle for Tarawa in November 1943.

Russian tanks and troops in battle, 1942.

lion's share of funds, did not support it, and universal military training got lost in the cold war shuffle. After all, who would need citizen soldiers in the short atomic war expected to be the future norm. For that type of warfare, highly trained specialists, not soldiers from the general population, would fill the need.

And finally, throughout the war, supporters of collective security talked of a "second chance" for a League of Nations type of organization. Idealists continued to believe that had the United States only joined the League in 1919 the Second World War would not have occurred. Realists continued to point to the weakness of collective security concepts and girded themselves for a new battle. In this they were helped by Roosevelt, who saw the evolving United Nations proposals as politically desirable, but who did not believe that such an organization would bring the millennium that its sponsers envisioned. The president thus based his approach on the future cooperation of the leading powers (the United States, Soviet Union, Great Britain, and China) with the United Nations becoming more a forum for discussion than the actual instrument for peace. Realistic in his appraisal that no organization would work if the great powers were in conflict, but unrealistic in his inclusion of China and even Great Britain, FDR was typically vague in his approach. Indeed, the United Nations concept was sold by its supporters to Americans in a millennialist manner that belied the president's intentions. His successor, Truman, was to support the birth of the organization and its idealist motivations, but would eventually turn to a nationalistic approach as the great powers' cooperation broke down in the face of irreconcilable antagonisms. Many Americans, misled by overenthusiastic promoters of the United Nations, found it difficult to understand why once more collective security had failed. Neither Roosevelt nor Truman had fully subscribed to its principles or let the American public know of their doubts.

The results of the Second World War are filled with ironies and paradoxes for the United States. Unrealistic hopes for a continuation of the wartime alliance dissolved and were replaced by a "cold war" confrontation, first in Europe, then in Asia, with the Soviet Union. Europe was the central concern of both great powers, and neither could seriously doubt the importance of that concern on the part of their opposition.

Because of that recognition, Europe was to remain divided along the territorial lines of May 1945 for the next forty years. Little change in the status quo took place despite periodic signs of serious internal unrest within the European states comprising both alliances. Germany and its future remained the key, as it has throughout the twentieth century. The Western alliance was more prepared to accept the possibility of a peaceful, democratic Germany than was the Eastern bloc. Troops and weapons, despite their high numbers and often high state of tension, were not used directly against each other. An important overlooked fact—that the United States and Russia have never fought each other in a war—remained intact despite the major interest of both powers in the future of Europe. In a status quo situation, with neither side willing to challenge the other directly with military force, both discovered that they did not have the power to change the basic military or political arrangements without the possibility of a major war. Both the United States and the Soviet Union had careful limits, despite their rhetoric, on their support of revolutionary currents within the other's sphere of influence. Too much appeared to be at stake to allow a repetition of the post-World War One period of unbridled self-determination. If Europe was in stalemate, it was also at peace.

The United States had a difficult time translating its military victory into a political one, particularly in Europe but also in Asia. In Japan the United States had almost complete control; there were no occupation zones, nor was Tokyo divided. This was made possible by the presence of American troops. General Douglas MacArthur, in a manner almost as imperial as the emperor, oversaw an occupation whose successes outweighed its failures. Japan was far better off having lost the war than she would have been had she won. Building on a democratic foundation, she was to become one of the world's leading economic powers without the burden of military costs.

A divided Korea was to bring a troubled legacy within five years, but it was in China that the United States suffered its worst setback in Asia. If indeed American-Japanese differences over China were at the core of the Japanese decision to bomb Pearl Harbor, and if Roosevelt really believed that a democratic China was necessary to the future stability of East Asia, as well as the world, then American military and

Chungking on fire, 1942.

political policies in China were at odds with these goals. American political policies fell between two stools; they failed to convince Chiang that he must reform his government to gain the support of the Chinese people and they antagonized the Chinese Communists as an increasingly viable alternative. Roosevelt tended, until quite late, not to lean on Chiang or tie strings to American aid. He also did not understand the intense hatred and divisions between the two Chinese groups. He supported Chiang enough to tie the United States to him but not enough to decisively influence the outcome in Chiang's favor. The movement of Chiang's troops in American ships to Manchuria helped Chiang in the short run, but led to an overextension in the long run. American military strategy, based on a Pacific island-hopping procedure, meant that the major struggle against Japan did not take place in China and that few American troops were in position there when the war ended.

It was paradoxically in Asia, where American interests were small in comparison to those in Europe, that the United States later was to fight two major wars in Korea and Vietnam. It was these two wars that strained and then broke the consensus ideology of American foreign policy. A more realistic policy during and after the Second World War might well have delayed that breakdown.

Selected Reading

James MacGregor Burns, *Roosevelt: The Soldier of Freedom, 1940–1945* (1970) is the most readable of the volumes on the Second World War diplomacy. A brief survey can be found in Robert Divine's *Roosevelt and World War II* (1969). Warren F. Kimball's *Churchill and Roosevelt: The Complete Correspondence*, 3 vols. (1984), offers great insight into the two leaders. Roosevelt and Stalin did not write their memoirs, but Winston Churchill's *The Second World War*, 6 vols. (1948–1953), is a masterpiece of writing, if not always historically complete. Dated but still useful is Herbert Feis's *Churchill, Roosevelt, Stalin: The War They Waged and the Peace They Sought* (1957). W. Averell Harriman and Ellie Abel's *Special Envoy to Churchill and Stalin, 1941–1946* (1975) places Harriman in a key position; Robert E. Sherwood puts Harry Hopkins in *Roosevelt and Hopkins: An Intimate History* (1950) in a similar role.

Various aspects of American policy are covered in specific monographs. Roger Louis' *Imperialism at Bay: The United States and the Decolonization of the British Empire* (1978) is a classic work. Christopher Thorne's three works, *Allies of a Kind: The United States, Britain, and the War Against Japan, 1941–1945* (1978), *The Issue of War: States, Societies, and the Far Eastern Conflict of 1941–1945* (1985), and *Racial Aspects of the Far Eastern War of 1941–1945* (1981), have a critical tone that stresses, especially in the latter two works, differences between the Americans and British. Two realist works by Hans Morgenthau and Anne Armstrong, respectively, are *In Defense of the National Interest: A Critical Examination of American Foreign Policy* (1951) and *Unconditional Surrender: The Impact of the Casablanca Policy Upon World War II* (1961). Theodore Wilson covers the Atlantic Conference in *The First Summit: Roosevelt and Churchill at Placentia Bay, 1942* (1969). *The Politics of TORCH: The Allied Landings and the Algiers Putsch, 1941* (1974) by Arthur L. Funk explains the invasion of North Africa. John Lewis Gaddis' *The United States and the Origins of the Cold War, 1941–1947* (1972) is an excellent work, as is George Herring's *Aid to Russia, 1941–1946* (1976). Akira Iriyi is original as ever in *Power and Culture: The Japanese-American War, 1941–1945* (1980). A brilliantly written book is Barbara Tuchman's *Stilwell and the American Experience in China, 1911–1945* (1970). Diane Shaver Clemen's *Yalta* (1970) is a good introduction. A different perspective can be found in Norman D. Markowitz's *The Rise and Fall of the People's Century: Henry A. Wallace and American Liberalism, 1941–1948* (1973). A small classic is Stephen E. Ambrose's *Eisenhower and Berlin, 1945: The Decision to Halt at the Elbe* (1967).

Books on the military in the Second World War number in the thousands. For our purposes the two most useful general surveys are B.H. Liddell Hart's *History of the Second World War* (1970) and Peter Calvocoressi and Guy Wint's *Total War: The Story of World War II* (1972). Paul Kennedy's *Strategy and Diplomacy* (1983) has an insightful chapter on Japanese strategy. John Toland's *The Rising Sun: The Decline and Fall of the Japanese Empire, 1936–1945* (1970) is a solid description of the Japanese position. Short but essential is Kent Roberts Greenfield, *American Strategy in World War II: A Reconsideration* (1963). Michael S. Sherry's *Preparing for the Next War, American Plans for Postwar Defense, 1941–45* (1977) is an important and revealing book.

Peter Wyden's *Day One: Before Hiroshima and After* (1984) describes how the atomic bomb came about. *A World Destroyed: The Atomic Bomb in the Grand Alliance* (1975) by Martin Sherwin should also be read. Robert Butow's *Japan's Decision to Surrender* (1954) is a valuable book about the Japanese. A controversial revisionist work is Gar Alperovitz's *Atomic Diplomacy: Hiroshima and Potsdam* (1965). David S. Wyman's *The Abandonment of the Jews: America and the Holocaust, 1941–1945* (1984) covers its topic in excellent fashion. Both Eric Larrabee's *Commander In Chief: Franklin Delano Roosevelt, His Lieutenants, and Their War* (1987) and Michael S. Sherry's *The Rise of American Air Power: The Creation of Armagedden* (1987) are superb studies.

Conclusion

The historical experiences, economic capabilities, and institutionalized methods of allocating power that determine the motives and conduct of foreign relations are unique to each nation. Despite oft-expressed arguments to the contrary, such dissimilarities, rather than similarities, stand at the core of international antagonisms. A national character, an outlook, a way of doing things, indeed, of thinking, mark each nation's conduct of foreign relations and distinguish it from others. Departures from such "traditions" are unusual, often temporary, and almost always done with a sense of uneasiness. Evolving circumstances, however, can cause a nation to change its understanding of its national interest, and to undertake actions that are only sometimes consistent with the traditional core of policy. From 1914 to 1945 the conduct of American foreign relations and national security policies did in fact change from that of an isolated, passive, and unmilitaristic power to that of a world power second to none. The traditional American urge to perfect itself in private, independent of all other nations, remained alive in 1945. But so too did the Wilsonian desire to remake the world in its own image and the Wilsonian belief that America's opponents were not only wrong but the source of all evil. Forty-two years later in 1987 the struggle between the traditional core and the new tendencies remains.

By 1914 the United States had evolved a certain tradition that included an independent foreign policy tied to a pattern of no alliances with other nations, nonintervention in the political and military affairs of Europe, a domination of the Western Hemisphere, and a hesitant expansion, **197** largely economic, toward the Pacific and East Asia. Protected by two oceans, allied with the dominance of a British Royal Navy that coincidentally protected American interests in a European balance of power that had favored the United States, and bolstered by the fact that there was a lack of strong competitors in the New World, American security interests were minimal. A modern defensive navy and a small, professional army sufficed. Neither military organization threatened any other major power nor raised the threat of a military class that aspired to domestic political power. A small corps of elite diplomats, leavened with political patronage appointments, carried out national policies unhindered by an uninformed, usually uninterested public.

The First World War and Woodrow Wilson presented the first challenges to this *fin de siècle* world. As the predicted short war turned into a bloody stalemate in the trenches of France, the United States moved from a benevolent neutrality to a declaration of war. Wilson, with the best of idealistic intentions, took his country into the conflict to make the world safe for democracy. Neither the first nor the last American president to seek good ends by bad means, Wilson believed that the power of righteousness, allied with the power of might, would bring forth a new postwar world of democratic nations that would solve their disputes, not through war but through rational discussions in an international forum supervised by an enlightened world public opinion.

The resulting disillusionment that came during the interwar period when the world failed to operate on Wilsonian principles led to a sharp swing to isolationism. That over-reaction, much like that of a small child who picks up the marbles and goes home when the game doesn't go well, failed to recognize that not only had the rules of the international game changed as a result of the First World War, but that the new players, such as the Soviet Union and eventually Nazi Germany, were playing a whole new game. The activist nations became those who not only discarded the old rules but, through their ideologies, created new ones. To them the uncertainties and hazards that made war so unpredictable and uncontrollable were not barriers but opportunities to be grasped and exploited.

Having entered the Second World War because of the Pearl Harbor attack, not because of an open, positive decision of its own, the United

States successfully defeated its opponents in the traditional military sense, but discovered that despite its enormous military power there were limits to its victory. Unlike 1914, the importance of maintaining a favorable balance of power in 1945 in Europe was much clearer to Americans. Security interests no longer appeared minimal. A small military was no longer sufficient. An unprecedented power vacuum existed with the defeat of Germany and Japan and the collapse of Great Britain and France. The United States, however, failed to translate its technological expertise, its economic power, or its military strength into meaningful political power. Contrary to much of its own rhetoric, and that of historical revisionists, the United States was a most reluctant imperial power in 1945. It would have preferred to retreat to its traditional solitude, but history had other plans for it; and even those did not materialize immediately. It is worth bearing in mind that, when the United States did have the Soviet Union at its nuclear mercy in the first years after 1945, it failed to impose its will on the Soviet Union so that Stalin could actually tighten his grip on Eastern Europe without a complicating American response. Perhaps one can hold that the Soviet Union would have behaved with equal self-restraint had the positions been reversed. Perhaps not. Regardless of that speculation, the United States did not, in fact, reach out to create either a political or territorial empire in 1945. Even in the economic sphere the degree of restraint was remarkable.

An unwillingness to think in political terms and a preference for legal or moral terms characterized American policies during the Second World War and after. Wilson, three decades earlier, had so conditioned Americans to think in terms of the rightness and wrongness of the policies of other countries that Americans failed to appreciate the cost of policies that produced moral judgments and legal decisions in a world in which power, not morality or law, was the determinant factor. The politics of power is always open to the art of negotiation, to diplomacy, but standards of law and morality are absolute, stress the principles of right and wrong, and make negotiations and compromise almost impossible. War too often remains the only possible settlement, for how can one deal with the devil? Americans might have heeded the advice of Karl von Clausewitz, the German writer on war, that "War cannot be divorced from political life; and whenever this occurs in our thinking about war, the many links that connect the two elements are destroyed and we are left with something pointless and devoid of sense." That divorcement of power and politics, of how to use power for achievable ends, plagued both liberals and conservatives, and remained the central problem of American foreign relations. It was events in the period from 1914 to 1945 that first presented the problem to Americans in its starkest form, and it was the same period that remained the foundation of twentieth-century American foreign policy and national security.

Index

American Foreign and National Security Policies, 1914–1945 was
designed by Dariel Mayer, composed by World Composition
Services, Inc., printed by Thomson-Shore, Inc., and bound by
John H. Dekker & Sons. The book was set in Times Roman with
Helvetica display and printed on 60-lb. Glatfelter.